Praise for *Rainbow Wisdom*

"*Rainbow Wisdom* is for allies to stand together to honor and respect rainbow warriors for exactly who they are. By showing the love and understanding we all deserve, we can collectively reach higher, better versions of ourselves."

BOB JOSEPH, bestselling author, *21 Things You May Not Know About the Indian Act*

"There's no better advocate for our beautiful community than Mischa Oak. *Rainbow Wisdom* is a celebration of our resilience, our strength, and our joy."

DARCY & JER, world-famous comedian couple

"An essential book for the troubled times we are living in."

TAMARA ADRIÁN, former Deputy of Venezuela's National Assembly; world's first transgender presidential candidate

"If you need a book to remind you about how to do right by yourself and others during these trying times, then *Rainbow Wisdom* is the book for you."

CHANDA PRESCOD-WEINSTEIN, award-winning author, *The Disordered Cosmos*

"Mischa Oak's heroic journey to becoming his authentic self by remaining teachable is now a gift for us all."

MARDI PIERONEK, trans elder, activist, and beloved social media personality

"The perfect blend of testimony, history, and antidotes to guide anyone on the journey to becoming more accepting, bolder, and more inspired by the joy and existence of the Queer community."

JAHQUÉ BRYAN-GOODEN, founder, My CRE Buddy: AI for culturally responsive education

"What makes this book truly remarkable is how it transforms lived Queer experience into universally human lessons. Mischa Oak reminds us that authenticity is a gift, not a liability, and that inclusion isn't about tolerance—it's about thriving."
JULIA RIVARD DEXTER, former Olympian; CEO, Shoelace Learning

"A wonderful and beautifully written expression of love, solidarity, and understanding for Queer people and for all people who seek the best for humanity."
LIBBY DAVIES, Canada's first openly lesbian former Member of Parliament

"A beautiful book with the brimming light of love and openness."
KALKI SUBRAMANIAM, Indian trans rights activist; artist; author

"This book isn't just for the Queer community—it's for anyone who wants to live with more honesty, courage, and care."
BARRY BRANDON (THE QUEER INDIGO)

"Whether you are Queer or an ally, I dare you to read this book and not be inspired by Mischa Oak's ferocious positivity as a strategy for thriving in these dark times."
RANDALL GARRISON, one of the longest serving out gay Members of Parliament in Canada

"*Rainbow Wisdom* affirms what the law—and our shared humanity—must recognize: that dignity, inclusion, and the freedom to be oneself are not privileges, but rights. Mischa Oak's voice is both timely and enduring."
PAUL RIVARD, retired Ontario Superior Court of Justice judge

"A masterclass in authentic living and a blueprint for how love can triumph over fear."
JONATHAN SANTOS SILVA, founder, The Liber Institute

RAINBOW
WISDOM

18 LGBTQ+ LIFE LESSONS FOR EVERYONE

RAINBOW WISDOM

MISCHA OAK

Cataloguing in publication information is
available from Library and Archives Canada.
ISBN 978-1-77458-554-2 (paperback)
ISBN 978-1-77458-555-9 (ebook)

Page Two
pagetwo.com

Page Two™ is a trademark owned by
Page Two Strategies Inc., and is used under
license by authorized licensees

Cover and interior design by Taysia Louie
Printed and bound in Canada by Friesens
Distributed in Canada by Raincoast Books
Distributed in the US and internationally by Macmillan

26 27 28 29 30   5 4 3 2 1

mischaoak.com

*Dedicated to the Queer heroes who came before us,
those we remember and those we don't.*

WANT TO FEEL REALLY GOOD
ABOUT LGBTQ+ PEOPLE?
TURN THE PAGE.

CONTENTS

YOU ARE A GIFT

FOR THE LONGEST TIME, I thought LGBTQ+ inclusion was all about equality and making my life the same as everyone else's. As a gay guy who often feels as though I stand out just by being me, I simply wanted to fit in. I dreamt of a time when people didn't bat an eye when I mentioned my husband or think twice when someone shared unexpected pronouns. I wanted to feel safe walking down any street without second-guessing or checking my surroundings first.

I just wanted to feel free—free to be myself.

I experienced a hint of that freedom when I became one of the first gay people in the world to get married on TV. In 2005, I was on a reality TV show called *My Fabulous Gay Wedding* at a time when only a few countries in the world allowed gay marriage. I was surprised by all the fan mail and recognition. We received letters from people in places where public declarations of gay love were only a dream. Most of the people who wrote those messages yearned for the type of support they witnessed from our friends and family. My husband and I were even recognized while wandering Times Square and on airplanes. People were excited to celebrate an era of new possibilities with us. I got to experience my fifteen minutes of fame—and the promise of hope for widespread change was confidence building.

But then that confidence began to dissolve. The more I looked around, the more I saw other LGBTQ+ people having a vastly different experience. At the time, I was working as a teacher, and I watched my colleagues, students, and their families face confrontation and cruel words—all because they wanted to feel a sense of belonging. When we put up rainbows to feel safe and welcome, we were met with backlash. People accused us of "rubbing it in their faces" or, worse, of "recruiting."

The experience of going from a public love story that was celebrated on television to witnessing the harsh reality of exclusion of people around me was jarring. I had been lifted up by acceptance, yet now all I could see was others like me being pushed down simply for existing—and I didn't like it. I had had a taste of what true inclusion felt like, and I couldn't ignore how painfully different it was for those who weren't experiencing that.

That's when I realized there is still lots of work to be done, and so LGBTQ+ inclusion became my life's work. For over two decades, I have been working to better the lives of Two-Spirit, lesbian, gay, bisexual, transgender, and Queer people. As a teacher, I spent seventeen years working to make the school system in Canada more inclusive. Eventually, my work morphed from teaching within schools to educating school districts and fellow educators, communities, companies, First Nations, and health care providers, and even guiding massive government projects, on how to better include LGBTQ+ people.

But I was still missing out on an important lesson.

It wasn't until I was working in a fly-in, remote Indigenous community in northern Canada that my outlook completely changed. I was working with a group of Elders—a group of loving and welcoming older women—who wanted to learn inclusion strategies so that they could guide their community in supporting sexuality and gender diversity.

In the middle of my workshop, one feisty Elder stopped me, stood up, and held my hands. She looked deep into my eyes and told me confidently, "You are a gift." It was a profound yet simple moment. She wanted me to know that my sexuality and Queer identity were valued.

There I was teaching them what all the letters in 2SLGBTQIA+ mean, but she was the one who was actually teaching me.

All of a sudden, I finally understood. Yes, being different is a gift!

As I kept thinking about what she said, I realized that humanity doesn't need to get its priorities *straight*, we're ready to get our priorities Queer! It was as though the clouds parted and I could see a beautiful rainbow. At last, I understood. Despite all the challenges we've faced, LGBTQ+ people are a gift to the world, here to teach everyone to live boldly, freely, and authentically rather than become whatever the world tries to force us to be. This was the beginning of my understanding of Rainbow Wisdom—the life lessons that LGBTQ+ people teach us all.

Queer people remind us that every person is unique, unusual, and different in some way. This book is about harnessing the confidence of individuality to make your life better—whether you are Queer or not. When we embrace change and diversity, we help the people we love become themselves. And when that happens, we can also embrace differences within ourselves. That's when every one of us can become the person we were always meant to be.

This is what LGBTQ+ Life Lessons are all about: ways to see yourself and the world in new ways, to be the best versions of ourselves possible—allies and LGBTQ+ people alike. The great thing is that everyone can learn from what the LGBTQ+ Community has discovered along the way. Everyone can benefit from Rainbow Wisdom, something the whole world could use more of.

The best gift you can give the world is to be yourself.

We Need This Book Right Now

Most allies didn't expect this to be a challenging time for Queer liberation. Many of us thought the era of marriage equality (same-sex marriage legislation) in North America, Europe, South America, and even parts of Asia and Africa meant the whole world was about to become Queer-friendly. Instead, the mid-2020s find us in a time of misinformation and hate-based targeting of Queer people.

LGBTQ+ folks are often painted as a threat, and Queer inclusion often appears to be up for debate, especially during election periods, as candidates jostle to get votes by turning people against each other. Yet I am confident that Queer people are a vital part of humanity's way forward, here to inspire us all to be better, fuller versions of ourselves, no matter who we are, no matter our identities.

As a teacher, consultant, and community organizer, I've seen what happens when the world leaves out Queer people compared with when we are welcomed in. I've watched as inclusion amplifies excellence, allowing everyone and their good ideas to flourish. Exclusion, on the other hand, tends to exacerbate poor health and self-harm in the people who are excluded. The resulting conflicts can then take a toll on the entire community, making life worse for all of us.

Everyone knows what it's like to be on a team that gels compared with one that is divided.

This book is an antidote to those who seek to divide and weaken us. It's offered to you and your communities as a blueprint—a way forward to create a community of harmony and possibility where we can all reach our full potential together.

No book will turn you gay or transgender, and that is not the intention of this one! What this book *will* do, whether you are Queer or not, is help you celebrate Queerness as a force of positive contribution to the world. If you're Queer, this book may give you a new sense of pride in your identity. If you're not Queer, it may help you become a Queer ally! These 18 LGBTQ+ Life Lessons will give you more confidence to take every opportunity to encourage yourself and others. You've come this far because you are looking for feel-good news and inspiration from the Queer Community. Whether you find yourself in a community of allies and Queer people or you are the only one you know, *Rainbow Wisdom* is offered as a guide to help you stay true to what's in your heart.

I've written this book for people who want to better understand and support the Queer experience—whether you want to stand with us more confidently and joyfully as an ally or you want to feel even better about being Queer yourself. Celebrating Queer identities can take many forms, whether it happens loudly in public, gently behind the scenes, or in the quiet of your heart. You are going to learn stuff about the Queer Community that you may not have known before. You will gain the Rainbow Wisdom to approach the world with more passion, flare, innovation, and liberty to be yourself.

I didn't always look at the LGBTQ+ Community so optimistically. I had to do some important learning along the way.

I Can't Believe I Said That

I remember sitting in Ms. Wilson's grade nine English class, loudly proclaiming that "all Queer people should be killed."

Pretty rich, coming from a gay kid.

Ms. Wilson lived with her long-term same-sex "friend," a common way to describe a lesbian life partner for those born in 1930. After my outburst, she gave me a knowing look I'll never forget—a mix of compassion and pain. I was essentially saying *she* should be killed. And, deep down, she knew that I was telling her I should be killed too.

I didn't actually believe what I was saying. I was parroting what I thought I was supposed to say to fit in. It was a defense mechanism—a toxic lesson I'd absorbed from the people around me. I thought I had to say bad things about Queer people so I wouldn't come across as gay. I never said anything like that again, because I felt horrible about it afterward, and Ms. Wilson's knowing stare made me feel even worse.

During my journey to self-acceptance as Queer, I learned that giving space to negative talk about the Queer Community only delays progress. It was hard to learn those lessons because almost nobody in the sheltered world of my youth had anything good to say about being Queer. What I heard was mostly nasty rumors and discrimination. I still cringe when I hear people spouting harmful misinformation about Queer people, because I know how harmful those words are in shaping how Queer minds think about themselves.

Fortunately, not all voices are harmful. As you read this book, you'll discover the many strengths of the Queer Community. Rainbow Wisdom enriches life for anyone open to learning. There's so much to gain from Queer perspectives—if you have the curiosity or courage to embrace new ways of thinking. Even the word "queer" itself has a fascinating history.

What Does "Queer" Mean?

The word "queer" first appeared in modern English in the 1800s and was used to mean "strange." Anyone who was *not* interested in the "opposite" sex was deemed strange and thus "queer." If someone didn't live in the same way as everyone else with similar genitalia as them, they were considered queer. So, it's not difficult to understand how, for many generations, the word "queer" was used as a slur often accompanied by fear, violence, discrimination, and exclusion. It was a word used to push people down and make sure they stayed there. It was a word that kept power in the hands of straight and cisgender people.

But something magical happened through the efforts of Queer liberation, beginning in the 1960s and continuing through the 1980s and beyond. Lesbian, gay, bisexual, transgender, Queer, intersex, and Indigenous Two-Spirit people who were activists and community members began to unite and work together to secure their collective rights. Through this advocacy, the Queer Community realized that being called queer (or "strange") wasn't a derogatory commentary at all. In a world with so many hangups caused by the pressure to adhere to straight culture, it became increasingly clear that being called different or strange was actually a compliment— and so the positive interpretation of Queer was born. From then on, the term "Queer" was reclaimed and became a significant source of resilience, confidence, and solidarity for the Queer Community, especially during the HIV/AIDS crisis of the '80s and '90s. This positive affirmation of Queer identity helped combat the stigma swirling around rainbow communities and brought people together.

Today the word "Queer" symbolizes the strength of being different and the joy that comes from being yourself in a world that doesn't always make that easy. "Queer" means being part of a global community of people who dare to be true to themselves.

Doing Better, Thinking Queerly

When people think of the Queer Community, they often get stuck in a rut, talking about the pervasive struggle of certain individuals to survive in a world that persecutes them. To be honest, Queer people are tired of that story! Yes, many of us have endured hardship and discrimination, but that is what has been done *to* us. Queer people are here to do their own doing.

Sometimes those who are against LGBTQ+ inclusion try to trick others into thinking Queer people want to recruit others into their community, replacing straight and cisgender people with "queers." But Queer people don't want to change people into anything they're not; we simply want to take part in shaping the world too.

The world pushes conformity on all of us, but *Rainbow Wisdom* dares each of us to embrace bold, joyful, and radically unique ways of seeing things for ourselves. What if people who are strange, unusual, unexpected, extraordinary, exceptional, and weirdly, wonderfully different are exactly what humanity needs to move forward and solve the challenges of our time? It's not about fitting in—it's about breaking free. It's about doing better and thinking *queerly*.

When you think queerly, you embrace your own uniqueness and that of others. Humans can do better, and we have what it takes to make our world better. We just need the audacity and courage to see diversity, trust it, and let it flourish.

Here are some ways to think queerly as you read through this book:

- Let go of thinking of Queer people as victims.
- Be open to doing things in new ways.
- Be excited to think in new ways.
- Get ready to learn from people whom you might not have learned from before.

Rainbow Wisdom is here to guide all of us as we seek to become the most authentic versions of ourselves. Because real fulfillment isn't about following someone else's script—it's about living as the person you were always meant to be. But let's be real: Challenging the status quo and showing up as your true self can seem like a big task! The good news? You don't have to do it alone.

Many of us know the magic of having a Queer best friend—someone who lifts you up, pushes you forward, and reminds you that different is powerful. That's exactly what the 18 LGBTQ+ Life Lessons are here to do. Think of them as your new friend, a personal cheer squad, your fearless sidekick, and your built-in support system, here to guide you into taking a leap into living boldly, unapologetically, and on your own terms—whether you're Queer or not! As you read this book, I hope you feel inspired by the Queer Community to live life better every day.

I invite everyone, regardless of sexuality and gender, to breathe fully, without the pressure of having to conform to how things have always been done before. Take a full breath—not the breath that others have *forced* you to take, but the one you really want. Your breath, your life, your mind, and your path belong to you. So let's start in Lesson #1 with what to do when someone dares to stand in your way!

A Note About Language

The word "Queer" is used throughout this book to represent the entire beautiful Queer Community of sexuality-diverse, gender-diverse, and gender-nonconforming folks who exist outside the experience of being exclusively straight or cisgender, or the traditional male–female gender binary.

If you don't like the word "Queer," feel free to replace it with LGBT, LGBTQ+, 2SLGBTQ+, LGBTI, 2SLGBTQQIA+, or another similar initialism, depending on the place you live or the context in which you are using it. When in doubt, you can also use the term "on the rainbow," which is a phrase I often use and another celebratory way of saying "Queer."

If you want to know more about the Queer terms used throughout this book, if you don't yet know what all the letters in 2SLGBTQQIA+ mean, or if you are unsure about the difference between sex, sexuality, and gender, please check out the **LGBTQ+ Glossary of Terms** at the back of this book, which defines all these terms and more.

A Message for Those Who Can't Be Out

Sometimes we simply can't be open about our true selves because it may jeopardize our safety, housing, or livelihood. If this is the case for you, please prioritize your safety and security—those are most important. Even if you must keep part of yourself hidden to survive, know that you remain just as beautiful and valuable as ever. Celebrate the honesty you maintain with yourself. Trust your gateway emotions—those gentle hints that reflect your authentic self—even if you cannot always act on them or openly share your identity.

Finding ways to let parts of yourself shine, even quietly, is especially important when you live partially in secret. You deserve to feel good about who you are, whether or not others can see it. You're still Queer enough, exactly as you are; there's no one "correct" way to be Queer.

If you can't find community where you are, I encourage you to seek out that community online. You belong to a global family extending to every corner of our planet. People who share your experience, and value you for exactly who you are, exist, even if they're not currently within reach. You're not alone; find your people however you can. If possible, travel to places that make you feel alive, explore literature, media, or online spaces that honor and celebrate your truth, especially if your immediate environment fails to reflect your beauty back to you.

Above all, know that you are loved, beautiful, and deserving of kindness, respect, and joy—no matter how hidden you might need to be.

LGBTQ+ LIFE LESSON #1
RAISE THE BAR

Skip the arguments.
Elevate the conversation
and stand by your values.

Save Your Energy for the Good Stuff

In the summer of 2023, much of the Western world experienced a rise in anti-transgender fear and messaging. Even in my usually mellow and inclusive hometown on Vancouver Island, transphobic community rallies started popping up. The organizers put up posters all over town that spread lies about transgender and Queer people. The posters were everywhere, and I was getting lots of calls from community members concerned about all the anti-LGBTQ+ rhetoric.

I decided to infiltrate one of the anti-transgender hate rallies to find out what was being shared firsthand. Queer people like me don't usually attend homophobic and transphobic rallies; it can be risky for our hearts, minds, and bodies, so of course I was scared to go. But I brought brave friends with me as backup, while my husband waited in the car in the parking lot in case we needed a quick getaway. We were afraid of the potential for violence.

We entered the dimly lit community hall where about thirty people had gathered. As we watched, one after another self-proclaimed "expert" got up to share rumors and non-truths in front of the seething crowd. I was surprised the audience believed what these people were saying, yet the crowd appeared to gobble up anything they heard, even if it didn't make sense. It was clear that they wanted to hear anything that justified their discrimination.

The angry crowd jeered that Queer people should be kept behind closed doors, like "a dirty secret," away from the public "so kids don't get any ideas!" And I watched in shock as the spectators craned their necks to better hear a disturbing description of mother–son incest that the reader claimed was found in an elementary school library. I don't know where they found that text, but somehow the reader connected it with a need to ban Queer-themed books in school libraries, even though the porn was clearly heterosexual. For the record, no school librarian would allow anything remotely close to the shocking stuff that was read out loud.

The thing is, Queer books don't turn people Queer. If it worked that way, all kids would grow up straight under the influence of the thousands of straight-themed books they encounter in their childhood. All I heard in my childhood were straight stories, yet I am gay because I've always been gay. No book would change that. And obviously, they didn't understand that an individual's gender and sexual orientation are a part of that person—not taught to them.

This room was the opposite of a think tank; it was a *fear farm*. In think tanks, people share ideas, experience, and expertise so they can come up with new ways forward. In fear farms, people breed fear and misinformation to stop progress. These were angry people clinging to a fantasy of "traditional values," which is another way to describe the cocktail of nostalgia, white supremacy, and evangelical-type ramblings that the rally evoked.

It was a lot to take in.

I spent almost three hours there, listening to the haters spin cruel lies about Queer existence. As a former teacher who had taught LGBTQ+ inclusion in schools, I tried to speak up and share the truth: It benefits us all to teach everyone to get along and support all members in our community, regardless of their identity. By making schools safe for Queer kids, we make them safer for all kids. Evidence-based, quality modern education must teach inclusion not just for Queer kids but also for those who come from families with Queer people in them.

I tried to correct wrong-headed claims that inclusion is about going into the nitty-gritty details of adult sex lives or convincing kids to secretly transition their gender expression. Inclusive education is about giving everyone the experience of being lifted up by society. But the people in this crowd just couldn't grasp the idea that kids need to know it's okay to be different so that they will learn to be kind to everyone. Instead, they equated teaching kindness with "sexualizing kids."

It was difficult to hold myself back from interrupting constantly. I did a few times, but I was shut down and told to rent the community hall myself. Eventually, things got too heated, the crowd swarming around us, yelling and pushing, so we left. The entire experience left me both shattered and more determined than ever to support Queer voices.

The commitment to fear that I saw in the audience at that rally made me realize that engaging in this kind of terrible debate wasn't going to get us anywhere. Radicalized haters are a lost cause, too far off the deep end of hate to waste precious time on.

Allies, Queer people, and other marginalized groups are exhausted by conversations with rabid discriminators because these exchanges are insulting and do not move us forward. To save ourselves and our energy, we need a way to sidestep these conversations in order to focus on community building and ensuring a good future.

And that's the LGBTQ+ Life Lesson for this chapter: Instead of descending into the muck of fear farmers, we need to save our energy, elevate our conversations, and *raise the bar*. And by that I mean we need to talk about important values and

Everyone deserves the experience of being lifted up by society.

goals for the future that we all believe in, instead of engaging in these endless and ultimately fruitless debates initiated by fear farmers.

Before we get into how to move forward instead of backward, it may be helpful to examine where all this transphobia is coming from, and why.

The Recent Rise in Queerphobia and Transphobia

During and after the COVID-19 pandemic, the negative spotlight on Queer rights was amped up as the fearful and the misinformed found each other online and in big numbers. These individuals used a catchy vocabulary of "sterilization," "secrets," and "grooming" to prime the rumor mill. People took the bait and started advocating loudly for the silencing of Queer voices, for blocking access to evidence-based mental and physical health care options, and for excluding Queer, and specifically transgender, identities from public spaces and public life.

This attack set up a political battleground, because many Canadian provinces, American states, and progressive countries had recently done the exact opposite, ingraining policies that welcomed trans and Queer students, families and staff into schools, workplaces, and community spaces. The haters and discriminators didn't like all this Queer inclusion, and so they placed evidence-based schooling and health care in their crosshairs.

Many of those who were against Queer liberation felt emboldened to take their discriminatory messages mainstream because they had amassed a large community online. Politicians keen to capture their votes heeded their call. All over the world, organized groups pushed governments and political parties to claw back inclusion initiatives based on the myth that youth needed to be protected from "harmful ideas" and "sexualization."

What a lot of these anti-Queer folks don't admit is that they are asking us all to discriminate. They push for schools and governments to forcibly out Queer youth, and they seek to restrict all mention of trans or Queer identities anywhere in the learning environment. What they call "sexualization" is simply teaching folks that you are beautiful no matter who you are, regardless of your sexuality or gender identity. It's not about teaching sexual practices; it's about teaching acceptance and kindness. Inclusion is about making our communities safe and welcoming for *everyone*.

By early 2025, the Canadian province of Alberta, the United Kingdom, and twenty-six American states, including Texas, Florida, and Georgia, had moved to prevent the doctors of gender-diverse youth from providing evidence-based gender-affirming care, even though every major medical organization, including the American Medical Association and the American Academy of Pediatrics, had opposed the bans on gender-affirming care for minors, and supported appropriately administered medical care for youth.

According to Human Rights Campaign, gender-affirming care is defined as "life-saving health care for transgender people of all ages and encompasses a range of services, including mental health care, medical care, and social services. Just like any other form of health care, gender-affirming care helps transgender and nonbinary people live safe and healthy lives. Trans people's health care is always delivered in age-appropriate, evidence-based ways, and decisions to provide care are made in consultation with doctors and parents, just like health care for all other people."

In the first moments after his inauguration as the forty-seventh president of the United States, Donald Trump entrenched transphobia in American national policy by stating that "only two genders" would be recognized by the United States. A scary era of legislated transphobia began, which will affect the livelihood, health, and safety of gender-diverse people across America and around the world. That mandated change will have drastic effects, including the limiting of employment opportunities for transgender people; the removal of transgender people from public life; the revocation or withholding of identification such as passports, resulting in the turning back at the US border of people whose gender identity on their passport does not correspond to their sex assigned at birth, and the trapping of gender-diverse people within the US who are now unable to obtain identification needed to travel; and the removal of funding for life-saving health supports and even anti-violence and anti-discrimination programs that help keep trans people safe.

In the context of a wide-ranging purge of any national efforts to ensure diversity, equity, and inclusion, the US anti-trans policy shift also halts all funding for any research into how to best support transgender, nonbinary, and intersex people. It erases their presence from all federal programs, including basic services, and even from national monuments; the words "transgender" and "queer" were removed from the national monument at Stonewall—the birthplace of the Queer Liberation movement. The plaque was censored so that it now reads "LGB" (lesbian, gay, bisexual) instead of "LGBTQ," thus erasing transgender and Queer identities from their rightful place in history. I'll talk more about Stonewall in Life Lesson #8.

Even though transgender people make up less than 1 percent of the American population, it appears they are receiving 100 percent of the hate of their national government. It's as if the battle against gender-nonconformity has become a national pastime.

Beyond trying to control the health care of others, transphobes continue to spread moral panic by propagating the lie that gender-affirming sex reassignment surgeries are regularly performed on kids. Worse still, a false narrative that these surgeries are being performed secretly and without parental consent continues to be parroted by politicians. In fact, there is not a single reported case of this happening in Canada or the US. But the facts don't seem to matter to those so committed to fear. Government-funded bottom (genital) surgeries for youth are exceedingly rare, not advised by global transgender gender-affirming care standards, and typically not happening to anyone under eighteen.

Still, government representatives in anti-transgender strongholds thought that because they had been elected, they could block trained medical professionals, the families of Queer people, and, most importantly, gender-diverse people themselves from seeking the care they want and need to be healthy. As of late 2024, nearly 40 percent of transgender youth in America live in states where it is illegal for them to receive gender-affirming care, including mental health supports. The fear, of course, is that the efforts to prevent gender-affirming care will soon be extended to include adults.

But these efforts didn't stop there. As of early 2025, fourteen American states had banned gender-diverse people from using washrooms that align with their identity. And in many American states, including Kansas, Ohio, and Tennessee, laws similar to Florida's infamous "Don't Say Gay" legislation have been rolled out. Even in the Canadian provinces of Saskatchewan and Alberta, teachers must now give parents at least thirty days' notice to "opt in" whenever anything LGBTQ+ will be mentioned in the classroom.

This is scary for Queer people, because all of a sudden it has become optional to accept Queer people or not. Queer people are being erased from the lives of young people under the government's direction. And it doesn't end there: Schools are becoming gender police too.

In those same provinces I mentioned earlier, and in many states including Arizona, Indiana, and North Carolina, if a student shares a non-straight sexuality or new gender identity with a teacher at school, that school is legally required to out that kid to their parents, regardless of the wishes of the Queer individual. That puts many kids at risk of homelessness and violence and forces many to stay in the closet. Many Queer kids aren't ready for everyone to know their true identity, so policies like these make kids more isolated and put them at greater risk.

Perhaps the topic that has gained the most attention and debate recently has been the inclusion of transgender women and girls in sports. This topic is usually framed as protecting AFAB girls from the brute force of those born with XY chromosomes. But this issue has also been completely blown out of proportion. For example, in 2024, of the 510,000 athletes participating in American NCAA elite college level sports, fewer than ten—yes, you read that correctly, fewer than ten— were transgender.

At the elite level, those against trans inclusion say they are defending "fairness." But the statistics that would point to transgender athletes enjoying a significant genetic advantage just aren't there. For example, the *British Journal of Sports Medicine* found that transgender women who completed more than one year of hormone replacement therapy performed worse than cisgender women in tests measuring lower-body strength and lung functioning.

I believe that most of the arguments about trans people in sport are nothing more than thinly veiled excuses for further exclusion and disrespect, so it's important we continue to approach these issues with compassion for transgender folks. The international sporting bodies that set standards for participation have some deep consideration to do regarding how they can best involve people rather than unfairly excluding them just for being transgender—an approach that needs to be based on the principles of inclusion rather than starting from a policy of universal exclusion. We'll talk about some approaches that might help them reach those goals in some of the chapters ahead.

As a former teacher, I believe the importance of sport in the lives of youth is less about winning and more about participation, gaining lifelong appreciation for fitness, and learning to play well with others. I would much prefer trans kids get the chance to play sports and cisgender kids get the chance to play with them.

This is not the first time social issues have become so polarized. The sad thing about polarization is that it slows down human progress because dialogue gets stuck in debates about ignorance and fear of change rather than solutions. Anyone who has had these kinds of conversations knows how draining they can be. And instead of standing up for what's right, allies of Queer people risk exhausting themselves in the process of fighting back.

The good news is that you don't have to fight with the misinformed to maintain progress.

Get Off the Ride

Conversations with people who are spouting discrimination usually don't go anywhere beneficial. That's because even the most well-thought-out and logical explanation will fall flat if the other person isn't willing to listen. They will say anything to justify their discriminatory mindset. Like the "chauffeur" at the transphobic rally I attended who insisted he had proof that politicians and schools were sterilizing children, or the granny who was sure every teacher and politician is a pedophile, there's no moving people who aren't willing to listen. They've been polarized into believing a point of view, a view they think they have to defend. And they are so ingrained in their attitudes that they will near-obsessively come up with an attack point, no matter what you say. It's like arguing with a merry-go-round: They keep coming back at you with discrimination worded in a different way, over and over.

People with this kind of discrimination mindset will often refuse to understand or change their mind even if you provide data-driven and life-lived anecdotes. I saw and heard this at the transphobic rally. They truly wanted to believe the lies. They were looking for an excuse to discriminate and hold back change.

People are uncomfortable with change because it disrupts how they understand the world and their role in it. If you're a progressive or an ally, you probably believe an inclusive society is everyone's responsibility. But some people believe things should just stay the same. *You* think about what we all can gain, together. *They* think about what they might lose.

After decades of exhausting debates with queerphobic and discriminatory people, I've learned that the best way to avoid burnout is to refuse to participate in their debates altogether. Instead, you need to change the level of the conversation. You don't have to get sucked in. You can get off that ride! Understand what they are afraid of: It's not you, it's change.

Aw, Honey...

Have you ever heard anyone make these kinds of statements?

- "I'm not racist, but ... "

- "You don't look gay."

- "I don't mind what people do behind closed doors, but just don't rub it in our faces."

- "Maybe we should have a straight pride parade."

- "But they're taking our jobs."

- "But don't all lives matter?"

If you're progressive, someone who makes these kinds of comments may be trying to stall your momentum. They want to trap you in a debate you didn't sign up for. In those moments when someone confronts you with stubborn discrimination, I'm sure, like me, you want to say, "Aw, honey... you have no idea what you're talking about." But that doesn't usually go well. Instead, you get sucked into an argument that makes more space for whatever fear they want to pass along.

You might spend lots of energy explaining why these kinds of comments are discriminatory or selfish, but such arguments rarely go anywhere. Whatever response you come up with, the person will inevitably riposte with an unreasonable tit-for-tat counterargument. For example, at the transphobic rally, a parent yelled at me that it was their kid's free-speech right to bully Queer kids.

One of the challenges of being a progressive-minded person is that people who are afraid of change are often attracted to you like a magnet. They will come up to you and say rude stuff just to break your stride. It's inevitable. Their arguments,

**Walk away from
the noise and
let your values
do the teaching.**

often just thinly veiled discrimination, are exhausting. And this exhaustion can discourage thoughtful allies from being vocal about progress.

Progressives burn out and then stay quiet. That's when the discriminator thinks they've won. And that's precisely why you need to know how to work to combat that silence. Queer people can teach us all a lot about how to deal with people who stand in your way.

Here's how.

Cut the Argument Short

When the arguing gets big, it can get heated. Everyone comes armed with anecdotes, facts, and conflicting data. In those moments, you might need a way out. Your new strategy is to *raise the bar*.

When you raise the bar, you sidestep debate and avoid tit-for-tat arguments altogether. To raise the bar means to elevate the topic of the conversation. Instead of fighting about their basic facts, you change the tone of the entire conversation by making a statement about your own values. A value is something big you believe in, like inclusion, safety, creating a welcoming environment, or justice. Instead of debating them, you will say what is important to you and what you are trying to achieve.

By focusing on your values, you will interject wisdom into any conversation. You'll also notice that talking about what you believe in instead of arguing makes for a much more satisfying outcome!

For example, instead of trying to explain to a transphobe that gender identity develops in our mind around the age of two or three, according to the Canadian Pediatric Society and the American Academy of Pediatrics, raise the bar of the conversation to a value you are upholding. Say something like, "I am looking for ways for everyone to be included," and then move on with your day.

Instead of getting dragged into a debate about trans people using the washrooms that align with their gender, raise the bar and respond that you want to "make washrooms safe and inclusive for *everyone.*"

By elevating your conversation and cutting the debate short, you'll save your energy for discussing these important topics with open-minded people. Seriously, just walk away and let the statement of your value do the teaching. You don't need to waste your time arguing with them anymore. If they want to learn, they will learn on their own, but at least you will still have energy left for the important stuff, like making a positive contribution to the world.

Sometimes, especially within smaller communities, you might forget there are others like you all over the world standing up for justice. Thank you for being a compassionate person! When you're feeling beaten down, please remember you are part of a massive global community that believes in goodness, kindness, and justice, regardless of identity.

YOU MAY NOT REALIZE it right now, but your ideas, words, and actions today feed into a web of conversations that will form the culture of the future. By being inclusion-minded, you are actively creating the space for the best that is yet to come. Without your conversations and actions today, tomorrow's progress will be delayed, so please keep it up!

In LGBTQ+ Life Lesson #2, I'd like to explore how we can all be better at supporting others when they reveal their true selves.

YOUR RAINBOW WISDOM TOOLKIT

Here is a list of some common progressive-minded values you can lean on, and corresponding statements you might use to *raise the bar*. Next time someone tries to suck you into a tit-for-tat-style debate, try making one of these statements instead, and then move on confidently with your day.

- When you want to celebrate humanity, try saying, "Diversity makes all our lives richer."

- When you want to foster collaboration, try saying, "Let's find ways to work together."

- When you want to encourage innovation, try saying, "Let's embrace new ideas as a way forward, rather than insisting on conformity."

- When you want to promote justice, try saying, "Our communities are stronger when everyone's needs are considered."

- When you want to appeal to people's kindness, try saying, "We all do better when kindness is our culture. Kind is the new smart."

- When you want to keep the dialogue open, try saying, "I'd like to find understanding rather than voicing my objections right away."

- When you want to highlight respect, try saying, "I want to build relationships rather than push people away."

LGBTQ+ LIFE LESSON #2

CONGRATULATIONS! YOU'RE YOU!

When someone
shares good news,
be a cheerleader
and focus on
the possibility.

The Big Reveal

I finally realized I was gay when I was nineteen, during my second year away at college. I hadn't spent much time in the closet, simply because I didn't realize I was gay for the longest time. It never occurred to me that I could be gay because I had never encountered anything gay in my sheltered, small-town, west coast Canadian village. I was never introduced to Queer people (that I knew of), and my community and family never talked about them. Queerness was invisible in my world. The concept of being gay seemed abstract. I hadn't met any openly gay people besides those very few on TV in the late nineties.

In hindsight, I realized I always had crushes on other guys, but at the time, the idea that those feelings were part of my identity never crossed my mind. As an act of subconscious survival, I was disconnected from my truth. I didn't want to stand out. I wanted to be accepted more than anything, so my brain never let me see what was obvious. I've heard this same experience of denial from many Queer people. We have the feelings, but out of fear, many of us ignore them as long as we can.

It took a night of drinking, with my best male friend, waking up with limbs entangled, to realize what truly turned me on. Suddenly, I got what the big deal with sex was! Sex was amazing. Up to that point I had been pretty underwhelmed with my intimate experiences with women. Sure it *felt* good, but I didn't get what the big deal was. All it took was that one night for me to realize who I was and that I had always been attracted to men. No more denial.

Right away it became important to me to share my true self with my closest people.

Now that I finally knew myself, I was ready to share my identity with the world. I bounced from friend to friend, eagerly sharing my gay discovery, only to face their constant downer concerns about my future.

There was always some part of their response that implied hardship, as if being gay was a life sentence or something. Even if they didn't bring up a big fear, like health, they managed to bring up a little one, like difficulties moving up corporate ladders. Their reactions made me so annoyed. How did they know how my life was going to go? They weren't giving me or the world enough credit.

The world is set up for straight and gender-conforming people. So when someone shares their true sexual orientation or gender with family, friends, their community, it is scary. It's a big deal for Queer people to come out because the exposure to the uncertainty of people's responses makes them vulnerable. They know they are shattering a perceived reality, so they do it with the hope that it's for something much better.

That's why the response of family, friends, and allies to this news is so important! When a Queer person finally shares their true self, it means they are less afraid of not fitting in than they are of denying themselves. They are beginning to free themselves of society's pressures that don't work for them! So, as an ally, when someone finally shines bright, you have a choice: You can be either a mirror that reflects that light back to them or a shadow that hides them.

Give the Gift of Hope

When I was still a high school teacher, I had an opportunity to give the gift of hope. I had this creative senior student who would make the most interesting art and say the most thoughtful things, but this kid always seemed sad. You know the type: always slouching, hiding from attention, trying to make the fewest waves possible.

One day this student came up to me. They had clearly been crying and appeared to be shrinking in body and soul right before my eyes. "Mr. Oak," they said, "I don't feel like a boy, and I don't feel like a girl. What's wrong with me?"

Immediately—with a big smile—I said, "You are perfect the way you are! That's an okay way to feel! There's nothing wrong with you." And then I asked, "Have you ever heard of nonbinary people?" They hadn't, so I suggested they go home, meet some NB folks on YouTube, and see if they learned anything about themselves.

The next day, when they walked into my class, they were seven feet tall. The once-shriveled shyness had transformed into a bright, confident person I had never seen before. They were chatting, bubbling, and participating. From that day on, they became a leader, launched an exciting art career, and never looked back. It was as if a light turned on in their brain because they finally found themselves reflected in the world.

When they shared their identity with me, I didn't respond with a doomsday prediction or assign them a problem. I didn't trauma-dump on them. I didn't drag them down. In that instance, I gave them validation and reflected their experience back to them in an uplifting way. I know that was a conversation that changed that person's life forever.

You have the same power. The power to change someone's life forever. What a gift. So next time someone shares

Be a mirror that reflects someone's light instead of the shadow that hides them.

assumption-shattering news with you, something tectonic that shifts everything you thought you knew, say something wonderful, exciting, and encouraging. They'll thank you and love you forever. You'll become part of their success story.

Be a Cheerleader, Not a Downer

Imagine a loved one comes out to you and shares that they are Queer. What would you say in that moment? It's simple: Say something great. I'm talking about a big, glowing, positive affirmation.

You're going to say something like, "Good for you!" "I'm so proud of you!" "I wish I knew myself that well!" or "Congratulations!" After that, you're going to keep saying positive things such as, "You're going to be so free to live life how you want," "You're going to have so much fun," or "You'll meet so many interesting people just like you."

Do you see the difference between being a cheerleader and being a downer?

This is your second LGTBQ+ Life Lesson: When someone shares big news with you—and I mean big, life-changing, life-rocking, massive news as in they are coming out—your new go-to is going to be to say something overly positive.

You have so much power in this situation. You have the superpower to lift people up and give them confidence to shine bright. The alternative, if you don't lift someone up, is that you might layer fear over someone, and that will dim their light, clip their wings, and delay their progress in achieving their full potential.

Even if your fear is real, it's not the time to discuss it. I'll talk about how to deal with fears in the next chapter. You can have a conversation about fears later if you really need to. All that person needs from you right now is to know you are with them, through whatever life brings their way. Tell them you believe in them, are proud of them for being themselves, and that true joy comes from authenticity.

Sounds easy, right? When someone shares their new life path, just say something encouraging! Whatever you do, just don't be a downer! Your validating words will amplify their self-worth. Your words, which cost you nothing, have the power to give someone the priceless gift of hope and self-worth.

This LGBTQ+ Life Lesson isn't restricted to when people come out to you. It could be any big life news they share with you. But here's the real life hack: You can use this LGBTQ+ Life Lesson on yourself too.

You Are Your Own Cheerleader

So now that you've realized you can be a hero in other people's lives by celebrating them, the real trick is to do this for yourself too. You have an incredible opportunity to be your biggest cheerleader. You deserve to celebrate whatever you are becoming at every step in your life's path.

Many of us focus on what we haven't yet achieved or compare ourselves to others. But when we see only what is missing, we miss out on witnessing who we are right now. Instead, try to encourage yourself. Celebrate who you are because until you do, you'll only be knocking yourself down.

If you realize you have a sweet tooth and have been beating yourself up about it, maybe it's time to own it and enjoy the treat you are going to eat anyway. Or maybe you realize you are a clumsy person, so instead of always calling yourself an idiot, give yourself a fun nickname to invoke whenever you make a fool of yourself. My friends love it whenever I make a "hippo" move! I'm celebrating my hilarious clumsiness.

It's way more fun and satisfying when you choose to celebrate your authentic self. It can feel silly at first, but that's because you are breaking the illusion of normal that has been built around your whole life. As you weave who you really are into your daily life, you will find a layer of happiness and satisfaction that wasn't there before.

What Queer people have learned is that the world might try to trick them into believing there's only one right way to be, but that's fake news! There are many beautiful ways to be, so instead of beating themselves up about who they are, they celebrate reality and own it.

Today, research shows us that replacing negative beliefs about oneself with optimism and celebration sets people up for success, especially if they come from marginalized or equity-deserving circumstances. Ellen D.B. Riggle's extensive research of LGBTQ+ success stories teaches all of us that when people believe in themselves, they are more likely to contribute to their communities and achieve personal and professional success.

So next time you're tempted to feel badly about yourself, visualize your life as a fashion runway and strut your stuff confidently instead. None of us can predict the future, so you might as well engage in a positive mindset from the get-go. It doesn't cost you anything, yet self-celebration can be priceless. Say something positive when you discover something unique about yourself or someone else! Instead of trying to fit into a world that doesn't suit you, just be you and encourage others to do the same. I want you to congratulate yourself instead of changing yourself. Congratulations, you're you!

I LIKE TO approach my work with a mindset of positive affirmation and celebration—even in the dark moments. And I hope you will take that same approach as you read the rest of this book. We are going on a journey. In the next chapter we'll take a look at what Queer people can teach us about challenging fear.

YOUR RAINBOW WISDOM TOOLKIT

Think about the times you shared big news with people. What did you want them to say? Something good, of course! Here are some suggestions on how to respond in those moments:

- When someone shares big news—like coming out to you about their sexuality or gender identity—respond with excitement and encouragement, not doubt or fear. Your supportive words can boost confidence and self-worth, becoming a pivotal part of their success story.

- Celebrate your own uniqueness and milestones instead of focusing on what's missing.

- If you have concerns, address them later. In the moment, be the cheerleader who lifts someone up rather than pulling them down.

CHALLENGE QUEER FEAR

Fear doesn't make
change wrong.
Question the fear,
not the change.

I Don't Mean to Say the Wrong Thing, but . . .

Some conversations stop me in my tracks—like the ones I have with good people who truly want to be allies but find themselves stuck and lacking confidence. I've met many people in this situation. All of a sudden, things in their lives have become complicated and a queer fear bubbles to the surface. They don't want to say the *wrong* thing, but they are worried and unsure.

Here is what this kind of situation often sounds like:

- A mom, her voice trembling, tells me she's worried her son might never grow up to kiss a girl because—wait for it—lots of the girls in his class are coming out as transgender. "Who's going to be left for him to kiss?" she asks.

- The mom and dad of teenage kids are beating themselves up, convinced they have somehow been *too* accepting. They are worried that creating an open, loving household, where their kids always hear things like "we're going to love you no matter what," has "accidentally" made their kid transgender.

- A feminist mom is trying to find the right way to phrase her fears without sounding like a jerk. "What if," she says carefully, "raising my daughter to understand the struggles of womanhood pushed my kid too far? Was I talking too much about how men are what's wrong with the world and my daughter was *really* listening? Did I make my daughter a lesbian?"

- A dad is concerned that his kid coming out at a young age is going to limit them in life. "What if he eventually realizes he's not gay but then is too afraid to come out as straight?"

- A grandmother who has Queer siblings she loves and supports is convinced there's a certain trendiness in being LGBTQ+. She is taken aback at how many *rainbows* there are in her granddaughter's class. "Surely there can't be that many Queer kids?" she asks me.

These situations reflect points in time when people have realized it's easy to say they want to be inclusive but, when confronted with change in their own lives, they discover it isn't that simple. It's more important to *do* the right thing than *say* the right thing, but that doesn't mean we always do.

Why You're Seeing a Lot of Change

If you feel like things are changing faster than they used to, you're not alone. That concept first became popular with Moore's Law, which explains long-term trends in how technology changes. In simplified terms, Moore's Law says that a computer's speed doubles every two years. The same idea applies to social change. And that is especially applicable to the visibility of diversity in humanity.

Before the 1900s, people didn't see as much social change because they were limited to their communities. They may have heard about social change through neighborhood gossip, or read about it in books, but they didn't always see it happening. But as radio waves, newspapers, magazines, and then TV signals connected more of the planet, people started noticing how diverse the human experience really is. As a result, more people learned to value that diversity. They may have become involved in movements like feminism, anti-racism, anti-exploitation, and environmentalism.

For other people, the opening up of the human experience challenged everything they thought they knew and understood to be true and best. They would say things like "Things used to be better in the good old days," or "Kids these days!" or "I remember when times were better." These phrases are still mainstays for those reluctant to accept change.

Then came the internet, which only increased our exposure to diversity and uniqueness. Now, each person has the potential to broadcast themselves to the world and welcome whatever and whoever they want (or don't want but can't help looking at) into their own life.

Instead of restricting ourselves to the stereotypes that dominated the media before the twenty-first century, the internet now allows us to curate the diversity we see.

Social media is a window into humanity's diversity. You can find your community, whatever it is, out there—even if you live in an unaccepting, vanilla, queerphobic, or isolated place. The world at your fingertips means you can connect to like-minded communities that can be a life-saver. Even if you're the "only" in your town, you're certainly not the "only" online. There's a whole community like you out there, ready to cherish you and value you for who you are or whoever you are becoming.

Even though we see social change and diversity more now, a lot of people don't realize this diversity has always been with us. Although it might look like a lot of change is happening, it's just the visibility of Queer people that has increased. Queer identities have always existed. It's the way we describe them and see them that has evolved. I'll explore some Queer history later in the book, but for now let's keep tackling the idea of change.

Blurring the Lines

Diversity isn't just a Queer thing; the whole world is having an identity renaissance.

For example, we are now more aware of those who are neurodivergent, people who choose to be child-free, straight men wearing makeup and painting their nails. And that is great news for all of us! When people around us are liberated to be themselves, it means we all have the encouragement to be ourselves too. As I once read on a fortune gifted to me in the desert at Burning Man (an annual gathering of over seventy thousand people in Nevada's Black Rock Desert, where a temporary city comes alive in a massive celebration of inclusion, participation, large-scale art, and creativity), "The best gift you can give the world is to be yourself."

As the unnecessary rules that constrain us are steadily erased, the boundaries between identities are also blurred. My favorite social media follows are those who blur the lines, such as men who are into floral arranging and sewing, femmes who are handy DIYers, and of course Queer people living uninhibitedly. Maybe you have your own heroes who are blurring the lines as well.

This increase in the visibility of liberation is not easy for everyone, though. A lot of people can't handle the change. For them, pop stars shaking their scantily clad booties in music videos twenty years ago was already too much, never mind

**Queer identities
have always existed.
It's the way we
describe them
that has evolved.**

the liberation of diversity today. People who can't handle the change in society want *certain* people to be *certain* ways and to do *certain* things. That predictability is comforting for them. The social norms and gender rules from generations past made it easier for some people to interact with the world because they understood it as a simpler place, which made it easier to define themselves within it. Basically, they liked it when things weren't changing as quickly because change makes them feel anxious, disoriented, worried, or even afraid—and for many, this is especially the case when the change around them is about the inclusion of Queer people.

But just because we're afraid of change doesn't make it bad or wrong.

Don't Fear the Queer

Wouldn't it be great if, instead of falling for the lies that lead to exclusion, we fostered an environment of empowering conversation around the Queer Community instead? If we have a system where we can have healthy, caring conversations, where Queerness isn't treated as a problem, then we can maneuver through any uncertainty that pops up for those trying to figure out their own life path.

As society becomes more accepting, there are more visible Queer people in public spaces than ever before. But this increased visibility also catches the attention of people who are fearful of this change. Many people are raised to think that inclusion threatens who they are. This is especially true for people who are raised to see all differences in humans as a threat. I'll talk more about how to quell these fears in the next chapter. But for us to move forward it's important to understand that this fear of Queer people is irrational and unnecessary.

Many people grew up not knowing Queer people even exist. Or maybe they were taught that Queer people are "dirty" or a "sin." Many were not taught that Queer people are common, normal, and as beautiful and diverse as the rest of us. For people in this situation, someone who is comfortable expressing their gender or sexuality in a way they are not used to can feel challenging or scary. And unfortunately, fear often stands in the way of acceptance.

Fear doesn't serve us. It just pits us against each other and puts our brains into survival mode. Fear pulls us away from what we really want to accomplish in our lives and puts us into a state of discrimination, a state that often gets justified as protecting yourself or your loved ones. How many times have you heard discrimination against Queer people justified as "protecting safety"? But just because someone fears change and explains it as being unsafe doesn't mean they have an excuse to leave people out. You don't need to be afraid just because someone has told you to be. Often, what a fearful person is selling you is flawed logic.

Flawgic

You've probably heard the rumor that there's a school in your community that has kitty litter boxes for students who identify as cats. You've probably been told about this *cat*astrophe by a friend or heard about it on social media. Maybe you're like the thousands of North Americans who even called local schools or wrote to community newspapers to voice your concerns. But this kitty litter story never happened. This story is a great example of *flawgic*, which is exactly what it sounds like: flawed logic.

In almost every community where I deliver workshops, at some point someone will come up to me to ask if I've heard about the kitty litter boxes for all the "cat kids" or "furries." They are usually implying that by accepting and supporting gender diversity in youth, we have gone too far and made it acceptable for kids to identify as whatever they want, including cats.

People are often surprised to learn this kitty litter story is an urban legend, a story made up and spread to undermine gender diversity. Even some of the most committed allies get sucked into passing on a rumor that upholds excluding trans and gender-diverse people without even realizing it.

The thing is, one's affirmed identity is not a choice—it is who you are. Identity is an innate and intrinsic understanding each person has of themselves. When people raise issues like kids "choosing" to identify as cats, they are validating the harmful misconception that being transgender is a choice. This rhetoric is not only misinformed but also discriminatory, as it dismisses the legitimacy of transgender identities.

The darker truth is that this kitty litter story is about a whole other reality in schooling these days: gun violence. This rumor started after some publicity around lockdowns in schools. Schools enact lockdowns—locking people into rooms—whenever there is a threat to safety. Educators and students need to be prepared to be locked into a classroom for hours at a time if there is ever a threat of a shooter or invader.

In preparation for the eventuality that students might be locked in classrooms for hours on end, administrators realized they needed to have a way for kids to go to the bathroom in an emergency. Hence the kitty litter idea was born. If a kid has to pee while locked in a classroom because it's too dangerous to leave the room, they can use a bucket that's been pre-loaded with kitty litter. The last thing anyone wants is a kid opening the door to shooters because they need to go to the bathroom.

So, sure enough, yes, there are places where classrooms have emergency stores of kitty litter, but no, there are no kids in any community going to the bathroom like a cat. That's just a flawgic-filled rumor. Do you think janitors would agree to clean up kid-used kitty litter? Of course not. It's all flawgic. And when people buy into flawgic, they buy into fears of others that are unnecessary. Instead of falling for flawgic that is used to challenge Queer people, we need to disrupt it.

The Flawgic Remedy

Everyone has unnecessary fears, not just hard-line conservatives. It's normal to worry about things, because we all want the best possible future. But the fear of diversity is an unnecessary fear. To get past the flawgic, you need to look at the source of your fears. Just as you were likely taught as a kid, you need to face your fears rather than retreat from them. Instead of automatically buying into flawgic that someone feeds you, you need to empower yourself with information and truth.

It's pretty scary that people will buy into a fear without challenging it. It's scary because these fears are then used to justify the denial of access for certain people to services they might need, such as health care. That so many people are willing to pick up and run with flawgic shows that a lot of us still have underlying discrimination that needs to be dealt with. If someone with discriminatory beliefs then encounters someone who feeds them flawgic that justifies their prejudices, they are way more likely to indulge them.

The antidote to flawgic is to seek information. Everyone these days is always talking about the importance of "checking your sources," but that is not as easy as it seems. You can't always find out where information came from. No one knows exactly where the kitty litter story came from, do they? Where does a rumor like that even start? And who has time for all that fact-checking anyway? No one!

Just because we're afraid of change doesn't make it wrong.

Falsification

A great way to find out if a story or rumor you've heard is based on flawgic is to seek out evidence that would prove it wrong. The act of seeking "the other side" of a story is referred to as *falsification*. It's the opposite of polarization, which is sticking to your side of the narrative no matter what.

The theory of falsification, also known as falsifiability, was first proposed by Karl Popper in 1935. Popper challenged scientists and mathematicians to make statements that could be disproved in the quest for true understanding. He famously used the example of disproving the claim that "all swans are white." For centuries, Europeans thought all swans were white. However, the discovery of black swans in Australia in the eighteenth century easily falsified that claim and demonstrated the power of Popper's theory. By searching for a contrary observation, the black swan, the widely accepted theory of the white swan was easily disproved.

Falsification involves seeking out what your opponent is saying in an argument and trying to understand why they think they are right. In essence, this means trying to prove yourself wrong, instead of looking only for what proves you right. You don't necessarily have to agree with the alternate point of view, but by genuinely trying to understand where the other side is coming from, you are more likely to notice any of your own flawgic.

This is a powerful approach, because it shines light on the rationale you are using to justify your own opinions. It means seeking truth rather than committing to being on one side or the other—a quest that is increasingly rare nowadays.

Falsification is powerful in a society because it is the only plausible way to include all people in decision-making and move toward a more harmonious society rather than a divided one. It is a conscious opting out of polarization. We can all employ this strategy in our daily lives to call out and eliminate our own flawgic and instead seek information and truth that unites, mobilizes, and benefits all people.

Facing Queer Fear

Occasionally, flawgic isn't the only thing standing in your way. Sometimes you're still afraid of something, even if you don't want to be. Many people have Queer fear because it's been so ingrained in our society. You can still challenge Queer fear, though. Looking head-on at something you're afraid of helps you figure it out. You need to find out if a fear is rational (something worth being afraid of) or irrational (not something you should waste your energy on). If you're ever faced with a Queer fear, try asking yourself these questions to figure out if it is a rational or irrational fear:

- Am I really afraid of this?
- If it came to pass, would the outcome really be a bad thing?
- Is this outcome certain?
- Is this fear realistic or blown out of proportion?
- Is this outcome really happening or have I heard of only rumored worst-case scenarios?

So what does someone do if they want to be inclusive but are still afraid of change? Remember that situation with the grandmother who was sure all those "rainbows" in her granddaughter's class must be a "trend" or a "phase"? Let's revisit it, and answer some of the questions listed above.

Is this fear realistic or blown out of proportion? Kids go through phases. Heck, all humans go through phases. So what? If a phase leads you toward a better understanding of yourself, your desires and preferences, that's wonderful. Think of a clique from your high school years. Perhaps it was the Goths, the emo kids, or the nerds. Did all those people stay the same? Of course not!

Is this outcome certain? No kid learns to be gay or transgender; it's part of who they are. They might do gay things or experiment with gender, but that doesn't define them, it's just part of their path of self-discovery. Even if some kids try on being Queer or a different gender expression on their path to fully understanding who they are, it's okay. No big deal! Queer people have pretended to be straight forever, and nobody cared about that! Maybe some of those kids in the trendy Queer group will end up being straight or cisgender after all, but we shouldn't be concerned about it.

If it came to pass, would the outcome really be a bad thing? An Ipsos poll found that across thirty countries, 9 percent of adults, on average, self-identify as not exclusively straight and/or as gender-diverse. That's about one person in ten. If we extend that average across the planet, that means there are likely more than 700 million Queer people hoping to find a community and be celebrated as much as everyone else. Shouldn't we be happy for them that they've found a sense of belonging?

There's no justification for excluding a group of people because a few of them might be trying it on for size. And even if it is the case that some people are pretending, that isn't a valid reason to stand in the way of being welcoming and inclusive to others. So, let's just live and let live instead of thinking we have the right to be way-of-life police.

LET'S LOOK at another example of a Queer fear from my list earlier in the chapter to determine if it's rational or not. How about the situation of the dad who feared that his son coming out prevented them from being straight in the future.

Is this outcome certain? People change the way they describe themselves all the time, and this doesn't apply only to children or adolescents. Adults do it too, such as when a married woman decides to go back to using her maiden name after having used a married name. So instead of worrying that a child's openness now will somehow stop them from evolving later, try using a perspective of curiosity or optimism.

If it came to pass, would the outcome really be a bad thing? If a kid is coming out to the world, they are probably a thoughtful, introspective, and brave individual, and those are all qualities we should celebrate. Their openness to change shows security and comfort with who they are. This is the kind of kid who will speak up if things shift for them, and that's a good thing! We should be more concerned that, by not coming out, they might not get the support they need to stay alive or cared for, rather than worrying that it's a phase or that they will miss out on kissing someone. See the difference?

AND FINALLY, here is another example. This one tends to create an enormous reaction given the political climate these days: Some people believe that Queer kids are accessing gender-affirming care by mistake.

Is this fear realistic or blown out of proportion? Well, the truth is that Queer kids don't get permanent medical help without sustained, careful screening from doctors, well-trained and compassionate professionals who make sure only people who demonstrate both real need and psychological strength receive treatments.

Is this outcome really happening or have I heard of only rumored worst-case scenarios? According to the international guidelines by the World Professional Association for Transgender

Health, most permanent procedures such as gender-affirming genital transition surgeries are reserved for those eighteen years of age or older who have demonstrated medical urgency. Youth are not showing up for hasty surgeries. Trans people must prove to doctors that they need support in order to be happy and healthy. Patients seeking medical or surgical gender-affirming care also have to prove that *not* accessing gender-affirming care would cause them harm.

Is this outcome certain? Even after all that rigor, and after a long wait time, a patient will need to jump through additional confirmation hoops, and will receive more psychological supports, all designed to make sure the patient is receiving the care they really need. Medical professionals think about the long term and discuss any surgery with their patient—and the patient's family if they are a youth—to ensure it's the best choice for the individual. These decisions should be left up to individuals, their medical care team, and their trusted loved ones.

IF YOU ARE BASING your fear on something irrational, or if you are arguing without understanding the other side, that's a sign you need to reconsider the question with curiosity and wonder what good can come of the situation instead. Queer people have always existed and always will; erasing Queer people from public life will not end diversity. So instead of silencing folks, let's foster conversations so everyone can find the communities, answers, and resources they need to be themselves and shine bright. We'll all be better off living in a harmonious society based on logic rather than fear.

Now you're ready for the next chapter, where we will look into the future with hope.

YOUR RAINBOW WISDOM TOOLKIT

Instead of falling for a fear, challenge it:

- Ask where your fear came from and whether it's based on facts or just rumor.

- Question any story or logic that demonizes Queer identities. Dig for real evidence instead of relying on hearsay.

- Try to prove yourself wrong by exploring opposing viewpoints—the act of falsification—rather than seeking only what confirms your own opinion.

- Understand that more Queer people are coming forward nowadays, not because their identity is new, but because they finally feel safe to be seen.

- Let go of fear-based thinking and focus on real, supportive actions that affirm everyone's right to exist as they are.

LGBTQ+ LIFE LESSON #4

SAVE THE BEST, LEAVE THE REST

Curate the future
of your dreams by
carrying forward
the best of the past.

Everyone Can Play

There are few things in Canadian culture as sacrosanct as ice hockey. A big part of that culture takes place off-ice, in the locker room, with pep talks and camaraderie. But that intense culture, including getting naked to change in front of each other, can be an intimidating nightmare for some people and the reason they stay away from the sport altogether.

In 2023, youth hockey in Canada faced a crossroads. Were they going to uphold the current locker room culture or adapt how changerooms work so that everyone could play, including trans and gender-diverse youth? There were kids who didn't feel comfortable showcasing their anatomical diversity to a roomful of people and wanted private changing options instead. This need was difficult to accommodate in the old arenas, where privacy was not built in, so changerooms became a flashpoint of conflict.

There were awkward moments, with some angry adults yelling that kids should have to get naked in front of each other. Things got weird, and that distracted everyone from the central point: playing hockey. And Hockey Canada faced a dilemma: Should kids have to undress in front of others in order to participate comfortably in the sport?

Hockey Canada wanted to do the right thing and make sure all kids could play as themselves. They envisioned a future where everyone was excited to play the sport. The organization faced a lot of backlash from traditionalists. Similar objections had been raised when the organization was trying to get women's and girls' hockey off the ground. Some traditionalists just like to keep everything the same! But Hockey Canada didn't bow to old-time pressure. Instead, they decided to embrace change and make locker room culture welcoming and inclusive for everyone, not just those with similar genitalia.

They came up with a game-changing solution. Instead of asking players to undress in front of each other, they decided that all players, regardless of their anatomical sex, should come to the ice rink wearing their base layer undergarments. Because players were wearing a discreet base layer that kept everyone's private parts concealed, the source of conflict and potential unwanted attention was removed from the equation completely. The players would still put on their outer uniforms at the rink, so they could participate in the encouragement and strategy-setting of the coaches, but now they could focus on those pep talks rather than their feelings about getting undressed. Problem solved; everyone could play.

The inspiring part is that this inclusive approach didn't just benefit genderqueer folks; it benefited everyone. Many kids don't feel comfortable getting naked in front of their teammates, never mind the unfamiliar adults in the room. All of a sudden everyone was benefiting from not having to bare it all just to play. Kids are no longer forced to get naked to participate, and adults aren't asked to supervise youth undressing in front of them.

You can see how some might have tried to paint Queer people as a problem, insisting that they were "ruining hockey," but Hockey Canada decided to focus on the best part of locker room culture and carry that forward instead. They left the nudity behind and carried the camaraderie forward. Win-win.

However, even with wins like these that benefit everyone, Queer people are often painted as a threat to the status quo that needs to be taken down. So let's look at that scapegoating and how to deal with it to create a way forward for everyone.

The Rainbow Straw Man

A straw man argument is a misrepresentation of something in order to make it easier to argue against. Queer identities get painted as straw men (or straw people) all the time. And Queer issues are like rainbow straw men. A rainbow straw man might look scary to some because they're bright, big, and bold. Take, for example, the recent popularity of drag performers doing storybook readings for kids at libraries.

There are people who use the notion of children meeting drag performers as a rainbow straw man. They probably think that drag queens are always dressed like those scantily clad or sexy performers usually reserved for adult crowds, and fear that's what is being shown to kids. But if those people simply stepped into a drag story time at their local library, they would see a kid-appropriate entertainer delighting kids and families, who are all thrilled to have someone teach the value of acceptance and the celebration of uniqueness—great age-appropriate lessons to teach children.

Now, if you are someone who values inclusion, you probably look at a drag queen or king as a performer, a clown, dressed up to entertain and illuminate the silliness of gender norms. After all, gender isn't so important that it can't be made fun of! Drag performers teach everyone it's okay to be different and expressive, and that it's no big deal if someone wants to step outside gender norms.

When we challenge gender norms, humanity moves forward because people learn that the world can change and that uniformity isn't a requirement for participation. Do we still want to live in a society that restricts people based on whether they identify exclusively as male or female? That sounds way too 1950s for me! But drag performers have become the obsession, the fight, the rainbow straw man that has to defend itself from an onslaught of irrational fear.

People fight rainbow straw men not just because they don't understand but because they are willing to swallow the age-old bait of queerphobia. Queerphobia, homophobia, and transphobia are a fear of or aversion to Queer, gay, or transgender people. Some dismiss the "phobic" label, insisting, "But I'm not afraid," but the terms also refer to someone who simply dislikes Queer identities, their visibility, and their inclusion in public life. Just because someone says they aren't afraid of something doesn't mean they aren't taking part in stopping it.

Let's look at how queerphobia over time has come to be part of our social fabric.

A (Very!) Short History of Queerphobia

Queer people have existed everywhere and throughout history, yet many people just don't know about it. Many people didn't even hear or see Queerness in their lives when they were growing up, unless they were fortunate to have positive Queer role models. The sad truth is that Queer history, or anything that might be interpreted as Queer, has often been downplayed, left out, or erased, so there's no way to fully appreciate how much of our history is truly Queer.

People will sometimes try to stop me when I'm talking about people in history who may have been Queer by suggesting that I don't have undeniable proof of their Queerness.

It's a double-edged sword, because it's practically impossible to prove someone's Queer identity without speaking to them, and when we can't speak to people of the past, there's no way to truly find out if they were Queer. Still, one thing we do know is that Queer people are noticeably absent from the stories of humanity, so there must surely have been more of them back then than we know of today.

For example, it's believed by many historians that Alexander the Great was open about his romantic relationships with men and that his chief war commander, Hephaestion, could have been his same-sex life partner. We know that Alexander the Great "conquered the world" but not that he was a true man's man! Why not? Also, many people are also surprised to learn that Queerness, under different names, was celebrated in some medieval Muslim societies and art forms.

You also may not know that Leonardo da Vinci, arguably one of the most influential thinkers that has ever lived, may have been Queer too. Some historians argue he may have been genderqueer, perhaps androgynous, or at a minimum interested in the themes of gender-nonconformity in his artwork. Although the veil of time makes it impossible to know if he was gender-diverse or not, we do have a historical record that he was accused of the crime of having gay sex. Leonardo's potential Queerness provides an intriguing lens through which to examine the shifting attitudes toward gender and sexuality during the Renaissance—a period when the Christian church began to intensify its condemnation of Queerness.

During the Renaissance (approximately 1300 CE to 1700 CE) the Christian church began heavily decrying Queerness as a "sin." Up until that point, even though those attitudes had been around for a long time, the Church had never systemically acted on them. So why did the Church now start enforcing the idea of Queerness as a sin? Well, some scholars

It's not canceling— it's choosing something better.

suggest that during the Renaissance, the Christian church was experiencing a drop in attendance due to ongoing waves of the plague. In short, they needed to start promoting heterosexuality to increase the birth rates of Christians to make sure there would always be enough people to preach to and pay tithes. Also, as scientific discoveries started offering more convincing explanations of how the world works, people began turning away from religion as their primary source of understanding.

The clergy realized that nothing drives attendance like hate, so many preachers began spinning intolerance from the pulpit as a way to get people in seats. Church officials hoped that by preaching against homosexuality, Christians would start showing up more; in other words, homophobia was part of a membership drive. Clearly, fear is a time-tested strategy.

However, it's important to note that Jesus did not explicitly communicate any intolerance toward Queer people in his teachings, though there are varying biblical and scholarly interpretations on that point. If he were alive today, I could see Jesus confidently preaching inclusion and joining Queer people at Pride celebrations. As the saying goes, he loved everyone and asked us to do the same.

Queer scapegoating strategies continued through the rest of the seventeenth, eighteenth, and nineteenth centuries, and well into the twentieth. After World War II, politicians led yet another attack on LGBTQ+ folks, labeling them as "Communists," an attack widely known as *the Lavender Scare*. The fear of being labeled a traitor/Communist was so intense that most Queer culture went underground during the 1940s, '50s, and '60s, because people were afraid they would end up as outcasts or imprisoned. This is a major reason Queer culture became almost invisible for decades, and why so many of us, our parents, and grandparents grew up in a world almost devoid of outwardly Queer people. Most of them were hiding!

In all these cases of scapegoating, Queer people were positioned by those in authority as a threat to stability, especially in times of great social change. Wars, plagues, and scientific advances were changing the makeup and beliefs of society both politically and culturally, and leaders took the opportunity to use Queer fear to consolidate their base of support.

I'll share more fascinating and little-heard Queer history later on, in LGBTQ+ Life Lesson #17. But for now, the point I want to underscore is that queerphobia has been a well-tested and unfairly used response to social change over the course of human history.

It's Not You, It's "Them"

It's a story you've probably heard before—minority groups being blamed for society's problems. One example of this kind of scapegoating shows up when people fall for "replacement theory." This is when people fear being worse off because they're sure a group of people is going to "take over" whatever they have, whether that's a job, a gene pool, laws, or their culture.

Scarcity (the fear of not having enough) is a universal human fear, so it's easy to activate that type of thinking in people's minds. For example, people might feel that there is more competition for the jobs they think they deserve. But instead of recognizing that everyone should hold the same right to compete for them, fearful people focus on what they perceive they are losing. Instead of blaming their governments for not diversifying the economy or investing in innovation, training, and education, a group of "others" is scapegoated instead.

Pundits and leaders love activating this fear with lines like, "They are coming for you," "You are under attack," "I will save you and stand up for you." They know a common enemy is the best rallying cry we've got, because once someone believes they have an "enemy," then everything becomes that enemy's fault. There's no need for critical thought, everything can just be blamed on the migrant, the Queer, the woman, the Black person, the person living in poverty, or whoever is positioned as the enemy du jour.

The story of blame intensifies, and all of a sudden a marginalized individual who likely holds very little power is cast as the source of all the hardship in the world. Talk about unfair. Many LGBTQ+ heroes throughout history have had to protect themselves from this kind of powerful oppression. It's time we recognize and speak out against this pattern of scapegoating.

Those who want things to stay the same often cling to this imagined scarcity fear instead of thinking about what the whole world could gain by working together. Rather than looking at how their own groups or leaders contribute to the problem, they blame others. We never think we are our own enemies.

I believe the Queer Community teaches everyone how to be better at accepting change. For many Queer people, change has brought more acceptance, visibility, and community. Sadly, for the hundreds of millions of Queer people around the world who haven't yet experienced Queer liberation, all they crave is change. The best way for us to help those yearning for liberation is to expand our mindset about what change offers. Thoughtful change doesn't mean everything has to go; it's helpful to remember we can still bring the best of the past forward with us.

Carry the Good Stuff Forward

The opposite of change is staying the same, and many people waste their energy trying to remain in idle, usually out of a desire for predictability and control. However, embracing change doesn't mean you need to abandon everything you love. You can adapt while still preserving the things that matter most. Change and tradition can coexist. Change is an opportunity to remove what no longer works and carry forward what does.

For instance, many religious communities have sought ways to become more inclusive of Queer people. Rabbi Elliot Kukla made history in 2006 as the first openly transgender person to be ordained by a mainstream Jewish denomination. He wrote what is believed to be the first Jewish blessing sanctifying gender transition as a holy act. This is a powerful example of how tradition can be adapted to embrace change.

Rather than blaming a minority group for "watering down" your culture, try celebrating what your culture contributes to everyone, and look for ways to include others in appreciating those best elements. For example, migration can be viewed as a way for newcomers to learn the best about their new home and for long-term residents to benefit from the fresh perspectives newcomers bring.

Instead of fearing that learning about others will somehow diminish your identity, teach others about the wisdom you value. Rather than erasing or resisting diversity because it feels like a wave engulfing your identity, focus on sharing and including others in what's special. You owe it to your ancestors and future generations to pass along what you want humanity to remember. And if you can figure out how to share that knowledge in ways that don't leave others out or require people to deny who they are in order to participate, then you're being truly inclusive.

The Queer Community offers a compelling example of carrying the best forward. Thriving as a Queer person often involves letting go of parts of beliefs and environments that

Keep valuable traditions, but drop what's exclusionary.

hold you back. Empowered Queer people celebrate and honor themselves, even when others don't. Many Queer people have had to leave unsupportive families and communities, and they've learned to embrace what benefits them out of necessity and an instinct for survival.

Many, if not most, Queer people grow up in places where people, friends, and family expect them to be straight or gender-conforming. As a result, they often venture beyond their original homes and communities in search of more supportive spaces where they can discover who they truly are. Those who aren't accepting and are left behind might feel they've been "canceled," but that is a victim mindset. When someone moves forward with their life, it is an act of choosing a better future for themselves rather than stagnating in an unhealthy status quo. It's not canceling, it's choosing something better.

Queer people navigate a world that assumes heterosexual or cisgender norms. They often need to break free from these expectations so that they can discover themselves, even if that means leaving behind familiar but stifling environments. Sometimes, they have to choose joy over the status quo. By doing so, they learn to take what serves them well, what they want to carry forward, and move on.

What will you carry forward?

Instead of being swayed by oversimplified narratives, those rainbow straw men I talked about earlier, embrace change and actively decide which aspects of your past you want to carry with you. The key is to stay engaged in the process rather than resenting the need to undertake it.

EMBRACING CHANGE while honoring the past is a modern expression of wisdom—an open-minded and optimistic approach that applies your core values in a rapidly changing world. Everyone can embrace change in their life. After all, the world is going to change with or without you, so you can either dig in your heels or jump on board!

When you view change as an opportunity to apply your wisdom—rather than a challenge to it—you transform it from something happening *to* you to something you are choosing to take part in.

Now that you're more familiar with the force of change, in LGBTQ+ Life Lesson #5 we will look ahead to how everyone benefits from considering the full story.

YOUR RAINBOW WISDOM TOOLKIT

Instead of fearing you might lose something when change happens, think about what your experiences have already given you, and continue to welcome evolution in your life. As you embrace change, try to:

- keep valuable traditions, but drop what's exclusionary;

- challenge misrepresentations of Queer identities by seeking real-life context instead of buying into scare tactics;

- recognize that fear is often used to blame minorities—call it out and reject it;

- consciously choose what you want to bring forward with you; and

- view change as wisdom in action—adapt without losing your roots, so everyone benefits from the best of what you value.

DIVE THE ICEBERG

When you face the
unfamiliar, dive deeper
to find the real story.

A Label Is Only a Starting Point

I was on my way to South Africa, halfway around the world, fresh off abdominal surgery. The doctor had made it clear I wasn't to lift anything weighing more than ten pounds. The catch? I had way too much luggage! So, here I was, a fit-looking thirty-year-old traveling with all this heavy stuff but unable to lift any of it. When I asked the elderly person behind me to lift my carry-on into the overhead bin, the looks I got from other passengers were priceless! To those people, I may have seemed lazy. But in reality I was just trying to keep my stitches intact and avoid a mid-flight disaster.

Humans tend to think we know what is going on just by looking at someone. But people are like icebergs: We see the part of the iceberg that is above surface level, and we don't always consider what's underneath. But the story of any one person is what is underneath the surface; that is their reality, their truth.

When we look at someone, our brain uses shortcuts, aka stereotypes, to quickly assume someone's story. For our ancient ancestors, stereotyping was a way to survive, a way to avoid getting a disease or even losing one's life. Anything outside the established community was a threat. The issue is that this threat-assigning stereotype thinking still lingers in your brain to this day. It's programmed into you genetically, but that doesn't mean it's always right. As Edward Said explains it, "Labels are not more than starting points."

You've probably had the experience of judging someone based on a stereotype. Perhaps it was someone walking down the street or who came into your workplace or a social gathering. Just by looking at them, you've already made up a whole story of who they are based on what they look like and how they act. You have had an emotional response to them without even knowing them.

Anyone from a marginalized group is familiar with this feeling of being judged. That "knowing" flash in the eyes of someone who has just met you inserts a demoralizing dynamic into your relationship right from the start and adds a layer of doubt to every interaction that ensues. You know you are being thought of as "different."

I once had a horrible boss whose eyes flashed with disgust when she realized I was one of "those gays." I guess my good style, charm, and cute mullet tipped her off. From the moment she met me, her barely disguised judgment filled every one of our interactions with distrust and discomfort. I was always left wondering, "Is she being rude to me because I'm Queer or because she doesn't like me?"

Of all the billions of stories and life paths out there, there's no way you can accurately predict who is good and who is bad. Here's a thought: If you might be wrong, then it's probably not worth wasting your time relying on those stereotypes that are lingering in your brain. Where people are concerned, instead of looking only at the tip of the iceberg, you need to dive down and discover what's underneath the surface.

In my advocacy work, I meet many people who feel justified leaving others out. They come up with all sorts of reasons to dampen, erase, or quiet diversity. But often, their reasoning is based on an opinion they have absorbed on their journey, a stereotype based on a tip of the iceberg. Somewhere along the way, they were taught something about others, and now they see only that in the world.

You See What You Want to See

Your brain has a knack for seeking out confirmation of what you already know. This is called *confirmation bias*. While you are going about your life, your brain is constantly looking for information to confirm the beliefs you already have. And because you are seeking evidence, you will likely find it. For example, if you think a certain group of people are bad drivers, you will likely only notice when someone from that group is driving poorly while simultaneously ignoring all the good drivers from that group.

The problem is that we are usually looking for only one type of evidence—the evidence that proves us right—and we ignore any evidence to the contrary. But if we neglect to search for evidence that would prove us wrong (Remember when I talked about falsification in LGBTQ+ Life Lesson #3?), we aren't seeing the whole iceberg. We miss out on seeing the whole picture because we are entrenched in preserving what we already believe.

But before you can try to see the whole picture, you have to be brave enough to see it. Like a little kid covering their eyes in a scary movie, at some point you must look through your fingers and find out what's really going on in the world. Many things you think you know about people are either incomplete or wrong. It's okay to be wrong. People make mistakes all the time; learning makes us human. This means every moment offers a new chance to do things better.

Taking the Time to Dive Underneath

When I first started my LGBTQ+ inclusion training work, I thought I was already an expert on the Queer experience, but all I really knew was what I had lived through. Over the last two decades, first working in the school system and then guiding organizations and communities, as I have learned more about the Queer experiences of others, I have been humbled by how much more there is out there to understand. For example, I've learned from trans and other gender-diverse people about how gender is one's identity, the essence of who you are, which is completely different from one's sexuality, which is more about what you seek in others (or not).

A really satisfying experience of diving below the surface was learning about the deeper meaning of Two-Spirit from Indigenous friends. As a settler and an ally committed to Truth and Reconciliation and who studies decolonization, I have always been excited to combine my appreciation for Indigenous teachings with my Queer advocacy work. For example, I've learned to appreciate that where I was born isn't just called "Canada." Vancouver is the traditional home of the xʷməθkʷəy̓əm (Musqueam), Sḵwx̱wú7mesh (Squamish), and səlilwətaɬ (Tsleil-Waututh) First Nations. In appreciation, I continue to seek ways to turn to and incorporate Indigenous teachings and guidance in whatever work I do.

When I first started my work, I thought that when someone called themselves Two-Spirit, they were sharing their Indigenous heritage and their Queer identity with me. I thought they were telling me that they are both Indigenous and Queer. But I've learned that is an incomplete definition. I now understand I was using a colonial-settler perspective toward Two-Spirit people.

Listening to Indigenous friends taught me that being Two-Spirit is more than ancestry, sexuality, and gender; it is a connection to something deeper. Each person I spoke with described being Two-Spirit differently. Some friends described it as a connection to Spirit, others as a connection to the land or the love of their ancestors. Universally, what they taught me was that being Two-Spirit is a gift, something to be cherished, celebrated, and "always welcome around the circle."

One of my dear friends, Mikisew Cree knowledge keeper Marie Marten, taught me that many Two-Spirit people don't identify as "Queer" and might even take the term as an insult because it is a colonial term that has been imposed on Indigenous people. She explained that, for Two-Spirit people, "Queer" doesn't paint the whole picture of depth and connection to spiritual teachings: "Being Two-Spirit is more than the fluidity of someone's gender and sexuality, it's about their connection to spiritual teachings. It's bigger than just me."

Many of the Two-Spirit people I have chatted with describe their identity as a spiritual gift and use that as inspiration to guide, care for, and uplift their communities.

Before colonization, many First Nations regarded Two-Spirit people as respected leaders who served as cultural ambassadors, healers, warriors, and strategists. Although not every First Nation recognized Two-Spirit identities, many did. Colonization eroded these traditional roles, stripping Two-Spirit individuals of their leadership position and undermining their significance. The introduction of homophobia and transphobia through colonial systems—such as churches and residential schools that violently indoctrinated the concept of sin—suppressed teachings that honored Two-Spirit identities, marginalized their contributions, and disrupted the social fabric of Indigenous cultures. Despite this history, the legacy and strength of Two-Spirit leadership endures, inspiring contemporary efforts to reclaim these roles and preserve their heritage.

Indigeneity and Two-Spirit identities are sometimes unfairly viewed as relics of the past, which makes it all the more crucial to recognize the Two-Spirit role models, leaders, and artists who shape communities today.

Dr. James Makokis is a Nehiyô (Plains Cree) Two-Spirit family physician from the Saddle Lake Cree Nation in northeastern Alberta. He is a respected leader in health care, combining traditional Cree and Indigenous knowledge with Western medicine. Known for his compassionate and culturally grounded approach, Dr. Makokis provides specialized care for Two-Spirit and transgender individuals, offering services that are both affirming and holistic. Patients from across Canada travel to his clinic, one of the few places providing culturally sensitive gender-affirming health care.

A nationally and internationally recognized leader and author in Indigenous and transgender health, Dr. Makokis gained national recognition with his husband, Anthony Johnson, when they competed on *The Amazing Race Canada* in 2019. Utilizing their platform to raise awareness of Indigenous and Two-Spirit causes, they won the competition and used prize money to further support their community and advocate for systemic changes in health care. Dr. Makokis's leadership illustrates how Two-Spirit individuals play pivotal roles in their communities, bridging spiritual teachings, tradition, and innovation to address contemporary challenges.

Another prominent figure is Blake Desjarlais, who was the first openly Two-Spirit Member of Parliament in Canada, representing the riding of Edmonton Griesbach. Desjarlais's work in the House of Commons was particularly influential, including efforts to reduce homelessness and improve housing options.

Makokis and Desjarlais represent a long lineage of Two-Spirit leaders who guide their broader communities. Two-Spirit individuals often transcend rigid binary gender frameworks, integrating the strengths of both masculinity and femininity. The focus isn't necessarily on who they have as partners, or what pronouns they use, but rather that being Two-Spirit is a spiritual gift. This is an important lesson that I would have missed out on had I not dived underneath the surface to take in the rest of the iceberg.

Even after taking time to listen and understand, I've realized I know very little. It's true that we don't know what we don't know. Admitting we aren't experts takes courage, yet this readiness opens us up to seeing more than ever before. It also takes bravery to learn from someone rather than assuming we already know them. With that bravery, we have what it takes to dive beneath the surface of the iceberg and explore what lies hidden beneath.

Learning from Each Other

We need to look beyond fear-based stereotypes and discover what is really happening in people's lives, rather than accepting scare stories at face value. Seek out individuals who are willing to share what lies beneath their surface—those who can guide you below the "iceberg" and reveal what truly sustains them. By offering genuine insights, they help create a more inclusive world.

Instead of assuming we know everything about someone or what's best for them, like a debater who only brings up points in order to win, let's create spaces where people can be themselves and share more about who they are. If a stereotype about Queer people is holding you back, that's your clue that

**The world is
more Queer than
we imagine.**

you need to get to know their story. If meeting them in person isn't possible or feels challenging for you, look for them on YouTube or social media.

When we respond to who people truly are instead of the narratives we've been given, we push society forward. The next time someone enters your life, try discovering what they need to share and how you can support their growth. Just as you are the expert in your own life, they are the expert in theirs. As the transgender advocate Kalki Subramaniam says, "Before we can fight for each other, we have to learn from each other."

For many Queer people, deciding how much of our true self to reveal is a constant balancing act. We're often assessing whether it's safe and worthwhile to be open. This can take a lot of energy!

According to current research, LGBTQ+ individuals make up about 9 percent of the global population. I suspect the figure is higher, as fear and social pressures still discourage many people from disclosing their orientation or full identity. In one-third of the world, being Queer remains illegal or criminalized, so it's clear that many people must hide who they are. But it's not only the law that keeps rainbows from shining brightly.

For instance, there may be more bisexual- and pansexual-leaning people than we realize, but stigma keeps many from discussing or disclosing their experiences. I've also noticed that there are plenty of self-identified "straight" individuals who engage in same-sex intimacy. Perhaps if such relationships weren't stigmatized, we'd have a better picture of how many people exist on a broader spectrum of sexuality and gender. Consider settings like prisons, industrial work camps, religious communities, and the military—places where Queer intimacy and identities often go unrecognized or unnamed. What I'm suggesting is that the world is likely more Queer than we imagine.

As attitudes toward gender and sexuality continue to evolve, I'm hopeful that more people will feel comfortable embracing their true selves. Perhaps one day labels won't be necessary. For now, however, all the beautiful 2SLGBTQQIA+ designations on the Queer rainbow help us express our differences, find community, and celebrate who we are.

Are You Safe to Be Yourself?

In my LGBTQ+ inclusion and allyship workshops, I ask participants to recall—or imagine—a time when they felt completely free to be themselves, able to take risks without fear of judgment. I invite them to close their eyes and truly recall what that felt like.

Go ahead and try it yourself. It's an important feeling to remember.

How did that feel?

When someone's identity is fully welcomed, they flourish. Without the freedom to share themselves completely, they won't contribute with the same energy or creativity. In that spirit, we want everyone in our communities to shine brightly. That's how we can create the greatest good for all. If people spend most of their lives dimming their light, they can't illuminate humanity's path forward.

It's not only Queer people who are forced to dim their light. This kind of self-concealment affects many, especially those whose identities aren't immediately visible—white-passing, mixed-race, and Indigenous individuals, people with chronic illnesses or certain disabilities, neurodiverse people, or anyone who thinks or believes differently. All of them wrestle with whether to show their full, authentic self to the world.

The Queer Community offers inspiration for creating spaces where everyone feels safe being more of who they are.

If you've been to a Pride celebration, you've seen empowered people celebrating their identities and community. If you haven't, I encourage you to join this celebration of diversity. Everyone is welcome.

Ultimately, we all play a role in helping others feel welcome, safe, and included. That means sending out signals of inclusion. Too often, only those considered "diverse" speak about diversity. But every one of us can help normalize visibility and celebrate the beauty of our differences. Inclusion is a two-way street!

Everyone Is an Iceberg

Queer lives often reveal something intimate right away, which may be why they can seem so different from the norm. Many people are used to staying superficial and blending in, but the truth is that everyone is an iceberg beneath the surface.

Think about a part of yourself you've been holding back. Imagine if others recognized how wonderful that aspect of you is—without judgment. Wouldn't that be amazing? If you want others to feel safe sharing more of who they truly are and to shine brightly, you need to model that openness yourself.

The Queer Community, in all its beautiful diversity, leads the way for anyone to fly their own flag—whatever that may be. Perhaps it's a quirky hobby, a piece of your history or identity, a passion, an interest, or a dream you haven't pursued yet. By revealing the parts of yourself that society doesn't typically celebrate, you create a safe space for others to shine bright.

When you celebrate the aspects of yourself that don't fit neatly into the mainstream, you encourage everyone around you to color outside the lines too. Wear the outfit you've always wanted to! Sing in the style that feels most like you! Try that new experience you've been longing for! Build a life that reflects who you are and express yourself radically. When you invite others to "dive your iceberg," you create an environment where others can too. Everyone has a story beneath the surface.

YOU OWE IT to yourself to get more out of life and see more in others than what your brain tries to trick you into believing at first glance. Now that we've explored ways to go deeper, our next step is to break free from the limitations of the categories we've all been placed in. That will be the subject of LGBTQ+ Life Lesson #6.

YOUR RAINBOW WISDOM TOOLKIT

Our brains often rely on stereotypes as shortcuts to simplify reality. Strive to learn from others rather than prescribing who they should be. Here are some ways to do that:

- Resist the urge to rely on stereotypes. Everyone has a deeper story hidden beneath the surface.

- Notice how your brain searches for proof you're "right." To counteract this tendency, actively look for what might prove you wrong.

- Approach people with curiosity; ask about their experiences rather than assuming you already know.

- Share more of your own "iceberg," by letting others see the parts of you that don't always show.

When you celebrate someone's full identity, you create a safe space in which they—and everyone else—can shine.

WHY FIT IN A BOX WHEN YOU CAN BREAK IT DOWN?

Queer people show
us that there is
freedom in climbing
out of those boxes.

Born in a Box

For much of my early life, I believed I was broken because I didn't fit the box of what it meant to be a "boy." I thought there must be something wrong with me because I liked running and laughing with the girls and chasing the boys, and I couldn't connect with many of the things other boys enjoyed. They felt my difference, too, and often reminded me of it.

As a child, I preferred designing patterns for furniture in coloring books over play-fighting. My favorite toy was a giant doll. I loved outfits more than weapons, and any soldier toys I owned ended up performing dance routines in my bedroom. But even though I craved fitting in, I never got the point of blending in. I've also always had a certain flair. I wanted to wear bold colors and unique clothing that some of my classmates teased me for. Most boys in tenth-grade rural coastal British Columbia weren't strutting the hallways in suede loafers, fluorescent-green sweaters, and bright white denim. I was dressing for MTV, not Highway 101, and I didn't understand why everyone was supposed to look the same.

Even as a little kid, I loved having good hair days, not out of vanity, but simply because it felt nice. I loved walking around in my mom's high-heeled shoes. I would sneak into her closet to grab them and then clop around the house. That was way more interesting than practicing kicking or throwing a ball.

Of course, there was nothing wrong with my choices—but I believed I was doing "girl" things, not "boy" things. It's disheartening to realize that as a child—who should be free to explore and enjoy play—I was already questioning why I didn't fit a certain mold. I thought I was broken because everything I had been taught about the "boy" box, other than the anatomy, didn't fit how I thought of myself. Had I grown up in a world without that box constraining me, perhaps I would have nurtured my creative pursuits sooner. Maybe I'd even be a famous furniture designer by now!

CHANCES ARE you've also had a moment where you felt pressure to hide or downplay some part of yourself that didn't fit other people's expectations. Maybe it was an interest, a skill, or even a role model—and someone along the way told you that thing or activity or person wasn't appropriate for "you." That's how life often works: We're boxed into identities before we have the chance to define ourselves.

I had a friend who dreamt of living in a van, traveling worldwide, and waking up to a new vista every morning. Their family and friends labeled the idea "odd" and urged them to abandon it. Out of shame, they did—and now they regret missing that opportunity to follow their passion.

I think of these boxes as a kind of social caste. They carry an implied ranking and a prescribed life path. Maybe you were taught that your "box" meant you had to accomplish something specific or carry on a family tradition. Perhaps your box is defined by your lineage, hometown, country, or community, which in others' eyes dictates your future or your worth. Maybe your box, in the eyes of others, means you can or cannot do certain things. Even your given name was chosen for you, shaping how the world sees you. Think of people named Karen in today's world—they must constantly navigate the memes and stereotypes attached to that name.

Not all boxes are automatically negative; sometimes a particular identity is a favorite part of who you are. But identifying these boxes can help you see which parts of you were decided by others versus the parts you've chosen yourself. You might relate to some of these statements:

- "When I was the only guy in the knitting club, everyone assumed I was just there to find a girlfriend, not because I loved knitting."

- "I grew up in India, so I have a different accent. So many people speak to me slowly because they assume I don't understand, even though I spoke English growing up."

- "Being tall doesn't mean I play basketball! I'm more likely to bang my head on a door frame than score a slam dunk."

- "Just because I have a lot of tattoos and piercings doesn't mean I'm tough."

- "As a woman in a male-dominated field, I'm either underestimated or hit on."

- "Just because I have a disability, it doesn't mean I need your pity or advice."

- "Being a lesbian in a small town means everyone is trying to set me up with their son."

- "I'm plus-sized, and I'm tired of being told what I should or shouldn't wear."

- "As an asexual person, people constantly say that I just haven't met the right person yet. But my sexuality is valid."

- "As a woman who loves video games, I hate being called a 'gamer girl.' I'm just a gamer, period."

People often box us in because it's a mental shortcut; like stereotyping, it keeps things simple. To reclaim your power, you have to break free from these external definitions and redefine yourself on your own terms.

The experience of growing up often forces us to break free of the boxes we've been placed in. At some point you do get to define who you are if your boxes don't fit. Think of the rebellious teenager, moving away from home or doing that thing that no one else in their world has done before. Or think of the Queer person who decides to seek community in a big urban center rather than being the "only" in their rural hometown. The act of unboxing ourselves is liberating!

Instead of corralling people into predetermined boxes, let's aim to expand our understanding so each person's "box" can reflect who they truly are. We have enormous global challenges—inequality, climate change, ongoing conflicts—and to tackle them we need to be open to thinking in new ways. We require innovation, not cookie-cutter repetition. That can happen only if we embrace the unique perspectives individuals bring when they're allowed to be themselves.

I've heard stories from supportive parents of Queer youth who describe their own "unboxing"—realizing their children weren't "wrong," but the world's rejection of them was. Many religious families once subjected their Queer kids to "counseling," harmful conversion "therapy," or lectures on "sin," only to discover these boxes were damaging their children's sense of self-worth and health. When parents reject a harmful "there's something wrong with my Queer child" mindset, they unbox themselves too, recognizing their responsibility to help the world accept their kids, not force their kids to fit into a world of intolerance.

Imagine if all that collective energy spent trying to force people into boxes went into shaping a world that celebrates people as they are.

Unboxing Yourself

What if we stopped defining "appropriate" ways to be masculine, feminine, Two-Spirit, or nonbinary, and simply let people dress, speak, or act however they choose—whether that's embodying spiritual and ancestral teachings, wearing glitter and high heels, or playing with action figures and toolkits? We can stop assigning stereotypes to every LGBTQ+ identity. We don't need to assume that if someone is flamboyant then they must be gay, or if someone appears butch then they must be a lesbian. Let's stop telling bisexual people they're "just confused," or suggesting trans people should express their gender in a way that suits others.

I don't mean that people who happen to suit their box are a problem. If someone feels feminine, masculine, or androgynous, that's wonderful! It's just that people shouldn't have to feel or act a certain way to qualify to be themselves. Removing labels and assumptions will make the world more vibrant, authentic, and compassionate for everyone.

Instead of assuming someone's capabilities or personality based on how they look or what boxes they check, we could focus on their goals and passions. Let's see people with disabilities for their own wishes, passions, and potential rather than defining them by stereotypes or limitations. We can celebrate the ways neurodivergent people think and engage with the world, and embrace their contributions. Letting go of our assumptions makes space for everyone to show up fully as themselves, unapologetically, and without barriers.

The same goes for boxes like race, anatomical sex, and nationality. We can reject the idea that racialized individuals need to "prove" their competence in predominantly white spaces and instead acknowledge the systemic barriers they navigate daily. We can question stereotypes like the notion that women are "too emotional" to lead, and instead

We all benefit when each individual is allowed to reach their full potential.

recognize that empathy and emotional intelligence are powerful leadership traits. We can reject the idea that men don't need to take parental leave and instead value caregiving as a shared human responsibility.

Unboxing ourselves isn't just about removing barriers, though. It's also about fostering individuality, so every person's unique humanity can shine. Every person checks more than one box, and it's precisely this complexity that sparks creativity and progress. Intersectionality reminds us we're never just one box; we are mosaics of multiple identities.

Intersectionality Shapes Our World

Growing up in Nigeria, Edafe Okporo faced life-threatening persecution for being gay. After surviving mobs and death threats, he sought asylum in the United States, where he spent months in immigration detention. Upon release, he had to navigate multiple, intersecting identities: gay, Nigerian, asylum seeker. In his memoir *Asylum*, Okporo details the systemic hurdles LGBTQ+ refugees face. He founded New York's first shelter for asylum seekers—RDJ Refugee Shelter—and ran for New York city council in 2025 on a platform of affordability, health care access, and dignified immigration. He reshaped his world and ours by unapologetically living as his full self.

Kimberlé Crenshaw first introduced the concept of *intersectionality* to describe how Black women can face compounded discrimination because of both race and gender. Each aspect of who we are grants a distinct vantage point on the world. I like the concept of intersectionality because it helps us see that each of us is more than just a single box. I see the overlapping intersections as opportunities for people to gain insights and perspective on themselves and others.

The intersectional identity wheel below shows you how everyone is so much more than one box, but rather a beautiful mosaic of infinite perspectives. Here is a brief description of those perspectives in the wheel:

INTERSECTIONALITY

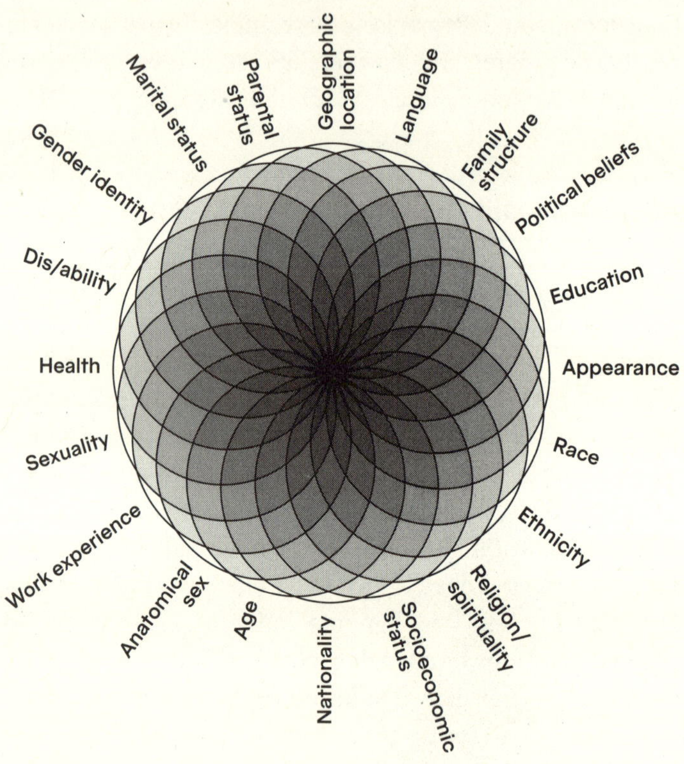

1 **Geographic location:** where we live

2 **Language:** how we communicate

3 **Family structure:** who we are related to and our roles within our family

4 **Political beliefs:** what we want our communities to be like

5 **Education:** what we have learned

6 **Appearance:** what we look like

7 **Race:** our perceived physical differences and shared ancestry

8 **Ethnicity:** our cultural heritage and common ancestry

9 **Religion/spirituality:** what we believe in

10 **Socioeconomic status:** our power in society

11 **Nationality:** the group of people we belong to

12 **Age:** how long we've lived, our stage of life, our generation

13 **Anatomical sex:** our genitalia, chromosomes, hormones, and DNA

14 **Work experience:** what we have done

15 **Sexuality:** who we are attracted to or not

16 **Health:** our physical and mental condition

17 **Dis/ability:** what our bodies and minds can and cannot do

18 **Gender identity:** our internal sense of masculinity or femininity in relation to oneself

19 **Marital status:** whether we are single, married, divorced, etc.

20 **Parental status:** whether we have children or not

The ultimate goal of embracing intersectionality is to move beyond rigid, "boxed-in" thinking and recognize that people embody multiple, overlapping identities. By appreciating this complexity, we can actively shape a more inclusive world rather than unconsciously reinforcing patterns of exclusion.

This shift empowers us to create the future we believe in, rather than merely replicating the limiting patterns of the past.

A great example of this is when governments and institutions include gender-free options on official forms, replacing "Mr./male" and "Mrs./Ms./female" checkboxes with broader options like "Two-Spirit," "Nonbinary," or "Other," or, better yet, allowing people to self-identify. This change reflects a commitment to ensuring everyone sees themselves represented. It means striving to include everyone rather than excluding anyone, much like when the Pride community adds another letter to the ever-growing, inclusive 2SLGBTQQIA+ acronym.

Shaping the world is another way of saying inclusion. It means deliberately moving toward opportunities to make life better for everyone rather than just a select few. When people don't have to expend energy hiding who they are, they can devote themselves to creating, innovating, and solving problems.

This is why I believe inclusion amplifies excellence. When everyone is unhindered and unrestrained, they are more likely to contribute to and shape the world around them. We all benefit when each individual is allowed to reach their full potential.

FOR HUMANITY to survive and thrive through whatever future is ahead, we need the best people to lead us, solve challenges, and innovate, instead of boxing them in. But we still have some way to go in breaking down the arbitrary boundaries of boxes and viewing the world as intersectional. And in the next chapter I want to explore a box that presents some of the biggest challenges facing us today: gender.

YOUR RAINBOW WISDOM TOOLKIT

Rather than telling yourself or others how to be based on identity, look for ways to *amplify* uniqueness so we can collectively shape the world around us:

- Notice when you (or others) say, "You should…" or "That's not how you…" and then challenge those limits.

- Shift your thinking from "Who doesn't fit?" to "How can we bring everyone in?"

- Ask, don't assign. Invite people to share their ideas and identities rather than telling them who they should be.

- Celebrate intersectionality and see people as multifaceted. Remember that every one of us is more than a single box.

GENDER-FREE YOURSELF

You are enough—
no gender rules,
no expectations,
just you.

Defying Expectations

In Japan, women are often expected to give up personal ambition, interests, and careers for the domestic responsibilities of motherhood and supporting their husband's career. But a quiet revolution is unfolding as more straight women are choosing singlehood over marriage and a traditional family role. These women, often highly educated and career-driven, are defying societal expectations that have long dictated their paths.

Instead of falling in lockstep with gender-based roles, these women are carving out new identities for themselves, challenging norms that have persisted for generations. They are choosing their own happiness over domestic servitude, and who can blame them? Instead of conforming to the conventional narrative of marriage and motherhood, these women are reclaiming their lives and redefining success on their own terms.

There are empowering stories of women holding solo weddings for themselves so they can have the experience of a wedding, complete with a reception, wedding cake, wedding dress, and bridal photo shoot, without the burden of a husband, while their loved ones get to participate in the commemoration of their special day.

The thing is, Japan is experiencing a demographic crisis: Not enough babies are being born. If more women could both follow their dreams *and* get married, Japan's population crisis could be abated, but the gender roles are just too restricted for many women to get on board. When a society forces women into choosing between a traditional role or following their dreams, that society loses out on their potential contribution. By letting go of this kind of gender norm, Japan would likely increase its workforce success and birth rate numbers. The entire country would benefit from a workforce enriched by the diverse talents and perspectives of everyone.

These Japanese women aren't simply defiant. They want to force a future where personal fulfillment and societal advancement go hand in hand. Of course, this scenario isn't restricted to Japan, but its example shines light on how a society where everyone is free from the constraints of outdated gender roles has real-world benefits.

Maybe you're ready to challenge gender norms too.

Questioning Your Gender Norms

I once met a grandparent who was mortified when I called their baby granddaughter "tough." I was admiring the kiddo for putting up with their rambunctious older siblings, but the grandparent couldn't believe I dared to call a baby girl tough.

"She's going to grow up pretty, not tough," they said.

"Can't she be both?" I asked.

We all grow up with gender norms. From a young age you knew exactly what men and women are supposed to do, the ways they should behave, and what they should value, likely through a combination of observation and education. Gender norms or rules perpetuate "wrong" and "right" ways of living. For example, maybe when you were a kid there were certain kinds of toys, games, or hobbies you were steered toward. Or maybe you were taught to like certain things because they were aligned with a specific gender role. Perhaps you went shopping for groceries with your mother. Maybe your father took you with him when he went to the car wash.

Here's a quick exercise that could help you zero in on your own thoughts about gender norms. On a sheet of paper, fill in the blanks for these statements.

* Women should _______________.
* Women are better at _______________.
* Women are worse at _______________.
* Women should not _______________.

Now fill in the same statements for men.

Among the examples you came up with, there are likely a few that are gender norms: rules and roles that we consciously or subconsciously place on people based on their gender. When I was growing up, I thought boys should like playing with weapons and girls with dolls. I was sure girls were better at art and conversations and boys excelled at sports. I believed that men built things and that women were better at cooking. How about you?

Let's go back to the gender rule statements you completed above. Since you are a confident ally, please consider people who are nonbinary—those whose gender doesn't fit either the male or female binary. Instead, they exist in an infinite universe of gender possibilities.

Now, complete these sentences:

* Nonbinary people should _______________.
* Nonbinary people are better at _______________.
* Nonbinary people are worse at _______________.
* Nonbinary people should not _______________.

Whenever we discuss gender, it is inclusive to include nonbinary and gender-diverse people too. Just like everyone else, they can face limiting gender rules. As you explore releasing yourself from gender rules, it can be helpful to see how you might be placing gendered expectations on others.

Remember the discussion of flawgic in Life Lesson #3? Well, gender rules are flawgic. Gender rules don't really add any value unless someone fits the role naturally. Instead of replicating gender rules repeatedly, I hope that after exploring how restrictive they are you'll be open to moving beyond gender as a way to categorize and constrain people.

A great way to develop your openness is to recognize that gender rules have always been in flux. Before the French Revolution, rich men and women both wore makeup, powdered wigs, and flamboyant garb. And high-heeled shoes, often seen as "feminine," originated in tenth-century Persia, where they were used by male cavalry soldiers to better secure them to their stirrups. And even in medieval and Renaissance Europe men wore skirts and hose to indicate their nobility, wealth, and status.

If you examine the traditional clothing of Indigenous and traditional communities around the world, you will see many that highlight the fluidity and functionality of clothing beyond gendered binary labels. Male Masai warriors of East Africa wear bright-red wrapped skirts and stunning beaded collars. And in Kanien'kehá:ka (Mohawk Nation) ceremonies, men wear skirt-like regalia.

However, gender norms don't stop with clothing; they go deeper, into how we are conditioned to behave. Many communities are waking up to the disastrous effects of teaching young boys and men to bottle up their emotions. So many men grew up hearing statements like "Boys don't cry," "Toughen up," and "Grow some balls." These statements can lead men to feel isolated, broken, and afraid to seek help when they need it, or to channel their frustration into aggressive tendencies.

The eye-opening documentary *The Mask You Live In* shows us how young men often struggle because society has conditioned them not to show emotion or vulnerability. One of the most moving moments comes when the filmmakers visit men serving life sentences in prison, who recount how emotional suppression led them down destructive paths toward criminal and violent decisions.

If we want the health of the world to improve, we have to stop teaching boys *toxic masculinity*. This doesn't mean that masculinity is inherently bad, just that the version that is taught to so many boys and young men is. The antidote to toxic masculinity is to teach boys it's okay to be feminine just as much as it's okay to be anything else. It doesn't mean getting rid of play-fighting or mechanical toys; it means a boy should be just as accepted as any girl in the room when playing with a doll. It means celebrating boys for being creative and sensitive just as much as we encourage them to be tough and strong. Leaving toxic masculinity behind means seeing that strength can take many forms. A complex aspect of gender is that masculinity and femininity mean different things to different people.

Your Sense of Gender Depends on Your Experience

Whether you visit a remote community in the Amazon, a village in France, a Polynesian island, or the busy streets of Accra, every person you meet will likely describe gender roles differently based on their lived experiences. Our sense of self, in relation to gender, grows out of how we've encountered and interpreted the world around us.

This is why it's odd that we try to impose gender rules on one another: We're all probably working with very different

The world is an infinite universe of gender possibilities.

definitions of what it means to be a man or a woman. Of course, there are dominant trends in how people think, but if you really get down to it, everyone will describe genders in their own way.

So here we are, using words like "masculine" and "feminine" to describe the world, while each of us likely means something different for each term. If you grew up in the bush with Cougar Annie as your female role model, you would have a very different perspective on what it means to be a woman than someone who grew up idolizing today's pop stars.

Because we can't define other people's genders for them, we have to let everyone define their gender for themselves. Individuals should be free to describe what it is to feel male and female in ways that make sense to them. We need to trust people to define their own gender because they know themselves far better than we ever will. As the saying goes, you've never walked in their shoes.

This trust is one of the main principles of gender-affirming care: I trust you to know and describe your gender in a way that makes sense to you. For example, when someone shares their gender with a gender-affirming psychologist or doctor, they are acknowledged and trusted, rather than challenged. We need to place power back in the hands of individuals, rather than allowing society to dictate each person's gender.

Genderqueer

Getting rid of gender norms benefits everyone, not just Queer people—but those same norms also affect Queer people in specific ways. Before coming out as trans, Elliot Page faced constant pressure in Hollywood to be more "feminine." Red carpets meant pressure to wear dresses and sport certain styling and makeup—whether he wanted to or not. But when he came out in 2020, the scrutiny didn't stop; it just changed. Suddenly, people were questioning his identity, picking apart his appearance, and holding him to a whole new set of masculine expectations.

Sam Smith knows that struggle too. Before coming out as nonbinary, they were told they weren't "manly" enough to fit the mold of a traditional pop star. Then, after embracing their nonbinary identity, the criticism flipped—people started questioning why they weren't "feminine" enough. The message was clear: Society loves its gender boxes. And if you don't fit neatly into one, lots of people don't know what to do with you and will tell you about it.

Both Page's and Smith's experiences highlight a frustrating reality: No matter where you are in your journey, there will always be people trying to police your gender. And that's exactly why breaking free from those expectations matters so much.

Many Queer people from traditional families speak of added complexity when navigating gender roles within the family. Responsibilities like caring for elders or children, and cultural practices such as wearing head coverings or traditional clothing, can bring up strong emotions for Queer folks. I'm not saying gender roles are entirely wrong; I'm saying there should be space for people to live outside those roles too. And these roles shouldn't be assigned based on someone's private parts or chromosomes.

Anyone in a same-gender relationship knows that rigid gender roles are often pointless. Nobody's genitalia, masculinity, or femininity will get the domestic chores done. If my husband and I believed only women are suited to domestic tasks, then nothing would ever get done! Anyone should be able to take on any role, regardless of gender, and feel good about it.

Feeling Your Gender

Gender euphoria is that feeling most of us know when we are having a really good gendered experience, like that glowing feel you might get after having your nails done, admiring your figure in a cute miniskirt, or flexing your biceps in the mirror. When you feel positive about a trait you associate with your gender, it makes you feel really good—like really, really good. It's why people get breast augmentation, hair transplants, Botox or fillers; why we wear flattering high-heeled shoes, tight tank tops, butt-flattering jeans or tights; or why we get highlights, a tight fade, or a mullet. All of these are gender-euphoric experiences—feeling ourselves in our gender.

Now, imagine never experiencing those feelings of gender euphoria. Imagine that you are not allowed to feel like your best self. That is *gender dysphoria*, the absence of joy that comes from expressing your most authentic, gendered experience. Imagine loving to get your nails done but being told you can never do it again. Or loving to wear makeup but being forbidden from ever wearing it. Loving how a full head of hair makes you feel, or how a flattering outfit brings out your confidence, and then being denied those experiences.

My friend and transgender advocate Grace McKenzie described gender dysphoria as the theft of those favorite fulfilling experiences—how transgender people feel when they are denied the ability to express and live their affirmed gender. Instead of experiencing euphoria, they are left with dysphoria: negative feelings that can arise during any experience that denies their gender. Those negative feelings show up in situations such as being misgendered or deadnamed, being forced to wear clothing that doesn't align with their identity or to uphold traditions that feel wrong, being denied an experience that reflects who they truly are, or even looking in the mirror and not seeing the version of themselves that feels like the real them.

We're All Transgender

Everyone wants to feel comfortable in their own skin. Throughout life, we all find ways to shape our appearance to match who we feel we are inside. Far from being mere vanity, these changes carry deep personal significance.

At some point, almost everyone wants to alter something about themselves to feel more authentic. Cosmetic surgery, hormone therapies, weight-loss medications, and even everyday choices like hairstyle or makeup can help us feel more aligned with our inner identity and more confident in our body. We all seek to feel comfortable in our skin, and these transformations, big or small, help us achieve that sense of authenticity. This isn't just about how we look to others; it's about harmony between our inner self and our outer expression.

In his illuminating TEDx Talk "Everyone Is Trans," transgender advocate Ian Harvie explains that when Caitlyn Jenner transitioned publicly, she faced relentless gossip and criticism for simply being true to herself. Harvie's powerful insight is that Caitlyn isn't the only "transgender" person in her family. He argues that anyone who modifies their body to feel more masculine or feminine is, in a sense, transgender too. By that logic, all members of the Kardashian-Jenner family (who have reportedly had cosmetic procedures to achieve a desired look) could be considered transgender. Caitlyn is the only one who *publicly* identifies as trans, but Harvie contends they're all essentially transitioning to feel more comfortable in their skin.

Harvie's overarching argument is that *we are all transgender* because each of us works to become the best, truest version of ourselves along the masculine-feminine continuum. Self-identified transgender people are simply the ones who openly recognize and name their journey. Indeed, whenever any of us changes our body to feel more like ourselves, in that way, we are all transgender.

This shared journey toward authenticity can be a powerful force of empathy and acceptance. When we support each other's paths to self-discovery and affirmation, we create a community that values and uplifts each individual's quest for their true self. So, let's break down the barriers of misunderstanding and see the common ground we all share. Let's support each other's journeys toward self-affirmation, recognizing that we all strive for a more truthful expression of who we are. By recognizing that altering our body for self-affirmation is something we all do, we can build bridges of understanding. It's about seeing our common humanity and the experiences that unite us, rather than policing each other and enforcing gender norms.

The Gender Police

In the 1960s the famous Milgram experiment revealed how ordinary people can end up doing harm when directed by an authority figure. In this study, an "expert" in a lab coat told participants to administer electric shocks to someone in another room for each wrong answer. Although the "victim" was only pretending to be in pain, many participants continued delivering shocks—even at lethal levels—simply because they were told to.

A lesser-known follow-up experiment placed victims in the same room as those administering the shocks. Scientists found that people were far less willing to harm someone when they could see the person's suffering. This shows how distance can make it easier for people to disconnect and follow orders that inflict harm against others.

Transgender people often experience similar disconnection from others: Many folks don't personally know or feel connected to anyone who's trans, so it's easier to dismiss, mock, or even harm them. A culture that normalizes mocking gender diversity can lead some to believe there's nothing wrong with discriminating against trans people. Pop culture has reinforced these attitudes for generations. Classic cartoons and old films frequently ridiculed or villainized characters who didn't fit strict gender norms, fueling harmful stereotypes. This transphobia still runs through media today.

Some anti-trans groups use the existence of detransitioners—people who reverse or regret parts of their transition—to argue that transgender individuals are being misled. However, many detransitioners say they were never given safe, stigma-free spaces to explore their gender in the first place. On top of that, actual regret rates for gender-affirming surgeries are surprisingly low—far lower than for most other procedures. A systematic review by the American Society of Plastic Surgeons shows a regret rate of less than 1 percent for gender-affirming surgeries. Now, compare that to these statistics:

- a 14 percent dissatisfaction rate for surgeries overall
- a 20 percent dissatisfaction rate for knee replacements
- a 21 percent dissatisfaction rate for corrective spinal surgeries.

Gender-affirming surgeries are scrutinized more harshly than any other type of surgery, despite having an extremely low regret rate—even lower than for tattoos (16.2 percent) or having children (7 percent).

Some may be surprised to hear that many detransitioners still support gender-affirming care, viewing their transition

Your gender
belongs to you.

as part of a broader self-discovery process. Their experiences highlight the need for safe, open conversations around gender. According to the National Institutes of Health, a supportive environment that "normalizes authentic expression of gender identity, affirms surgical goals without judgment, and destigmatizes the role of mental health" is key to minimizing regret.

What's often overlooked in the conversation about detransitioners is that many who regret surgical transition don't regret the act of changing their body; they regret the rejection, the stigma, the lack of acceptance they faced afterward. Their stories aren't a reason to silence conversations about transitioning—they're a reason to expand them. We need more support, more understanding, and more space for honest, compassionate dialogue. When anti-trans voices shut down these conversations, confusion and fear grow, creating more uncertainty and possibly, eventually, more detransitioners. Nobody wants regret. Talking about gender doesn't make anyone trans—it just helps people figure out who they really are. Anti-LGBTQ+ rhetoric often tries to erase these communities based on the false idea that identities are "contagious." In reality, hearing about diverse identities can help people who feel alone realize they aren't isolated or "wrong." Diversity has always existed. Denying it only causes more harm. That's why the visible work of trans advocates is crucial. It's much harder to hate or harm people when you truly know and recognize their humanity.

There's also an incorrect underlying belief held by many who oppose gender-affirming surgeries for trans people: They mistakenly assume that the goal of every trans person is to modify parts of their body, when the truth is that some will choose to change parts of themselves and some won't. Plenty of trans and gender-diverse people are perfectly content with their name, appearance, and anatomy, and others aren't. The thing is, there's no one "correct" way to be trans. We shouldn't care what people do to feel most like themselves. The important thing is that we're all free to make those choices for ourselves.

Queerness and gender diversity give everyone permission to express themselves more freely. Your gender belongs to you—live it and love it. Let go of rigid rules and let your self-expression shine. A world where anyone can be who they want to be—man, woman, Two-Spirit, nonbinary, or anything else—is a healthier, happier world for us all.

You deserve to love yourself, no matter who you are. Whether you're a "tough guy" who wants to dance and arrange flowers or an "elegant femme" who wants to get your hands dirty, you should feel free to do so without apology. Reclaiming gendered language for everyone (calling a man "sparkly" or a woman "macho," for instance) helps break down those restrictive boxes.

THERE'S NO RIGHT WAY to be a man, a woman, Two-Spirit, nonbinary, or whichever beautiful iteration of human being you are. You know your gender better than anyone. Liberate yourself and liberate those around you. It's going to be so much fun. And speaking of fun, it's the greatest Queer gift of all, and we'll discuss that in LGBTQ+ Life Lesson #8.

YOUR RAINBOW WISDOM TOOLKIT

No one should have to be "man enough" or "woman enough." There's no correct way to express or live one's gender. Here are some ways to gender-free yourself:

- Avoid "should" statements when it comes to gender, for both yourself and others.

- Be open to letting others define their gender for themselves.

- Be supportive when someone expresses gender in ways that work for them.

- Extend previously gendered language or rules to everyone.

JOY IS YOUR SECRET WEAPON

Queer communities
show us how celebration
and joy fuel resilience
and progress.

Stonewall Was a Riot

In the 1960s in major North American cities, Queer people would often gather in underground nightclubs and bars to celebrate life, dance, and freedom. Unfortunately, the police were never far away, constantly raiding the venues, and photographing and publishing the photos and names of Queer people they arrested. It was their version of doxing, intimidating people through shame and violating their privacy.

In the early hours of June 28, 1969, after yet another police raid, the Queer patrons of the Stonewall Inn in Greenwich Village, Manhattan, finally had enough and they fought back. There are many accounts of how the Stonewall Riots started, including that the uprising was sparked when a detained woman, likely a lesbian or trans woman, fought back and smashed her way out of a police car. Legend has it that she rocked the police car so hard that she was able to bust out.

The exact identity of the woman who was the catalyst for the riots is debated. However, some firsthand eye-witness accounts say that it was a lesbian in handcuffs, believed to be Stormé DeLarverie, a biracial lesbian and drag king, who resisted, fought back against four police officers herself, and prompted the riots. Reports say that she yelled out to the crowd gathering, "Why don't you guys do something?"

Whatever the catalyst, the crowd that had gathered erupted in solidarity. This turning point is considered by many to be the beginning of the modern Queer Liberation movement. The police were so scared by the unexpected stance that they barricaded themselves inside the Stonewall Inn. Six days of violent confrontation between the LGBTQ+ community and the police followed.

The riots were both intense and characteristically Queer. Police turned hoses on the protesters, while Queer cheerleaders shouted bawdy remixes of New York City schoolgirl songs and formed high-kicking chorus-style lines in front of the officers. Firebombs were hurled into the bar as demonstrators shouted, "Fag power!" "Liberate the bar!" and "We're the Pink Panthers!" Chaos erupted—windows were shattered, parking meters were uprooted, and coins and bottles rained down. Frightened and enraged police clashed with the crowd; arrests were made. Protesters sang "We Shall Overcome" in a campy, theatrical style, punctuated by a drag queen striking a police officer with her purse.

Marsha P. Johnson, a Black transgender woman (although the term "transgender" wasn't widely used in Marsha's time) and drag queen, was among the first to resist, and she became a symbol of defiance and hope for her joyous and triumphant stance. There are reports that she was among the first to fight back, throwing a shot glass at police officers and breaking a mirror within the Stonewall. She maintained her resistance outside on Christopher Street, and there are reports of her, along with her other drag, trans, and Queer friends, fighting back with utmost passion, climbing lampposts to launch heavy projectiles onto police cars to scare them away.

Those riots eventually morphed into protest, including sit-ins and the first Pride parades. And Marsha was a constant presence for all of it. Rather than being downtrodden or broken, Marsha did what she did best. For two decades, she would don her trademark flower crown, her most vibrant attire, and march in the streets along with her Queer Community. Even though she had little money and was living in harsh conditions, she used her visibility as a symbol of joyful resilience and celebration. In salute to her confidence, she added the "P." to her name, which stands for "Pay It No Mind." Today, the Pride movement continues to protest through joy, celebration, and fearlessness. During Pride, the Queer Community unites and says confidently, "You can try to come for us, but you will never steal our joy."

For Marsha, drag wasn't just a performance—it was an act of joyful defiance. By embracing her identity so fully, she created joy for herself and others in a world that was trying to erase people like her. In the face of violence and discrimination, she used her drag to spread confidence and happiness. That joy sustained her through decades of activism, making her an enduring symbol of resistance for the LGBTQ+ community.

For those of us who dream and work for a better, more inclusive and sustainable future, the journey can be exhausting. When you want the world to be better, those goals sometimes feel heavy and far away. Queer people know this feeling well, but we've learned that joy is our best weapon to keep going. Joy lifts us up and moves us all forward. Queer joy is a pedestal we can all reach toward.

Joy as a Catalyst

In the story of Queer liberation, one tool has proved as powerful as any protest: laughter. Comedy has been a weapon for LGBTQ+ people to fight back against discrimination, ignorance, and fear, especially in the face of conservative forces like the "Moral Majority" homophobia wave of the 1960s and '70s. But it wasn't all jokes. Sometimes, being visible and joyful was the most revolutionary act of all.

Many lesbians have used humor as a path to pave the way for the rest of the Queer Community. Lesbians were often seen as less "threatening" than other Queer folks, so many of them leaned into their identities to deflect attention. They used their visibility to uplift more marginalized individuals such as gay men, transgender folks, and others who were often more harshly policed.

Without lesbian visibility, the Queer Movement wouldn't be what it is today. In 1955, Del Martin and Phyllis Lyon co-founded the Daughters of Bilitis, the first US lesbian civil rights group. It started as a social alternative to lesbian bars, which were frequently raided by police, but soon grew into a key political force. By coming out publicly, Martin and Lyon made it easier for countless Queer people to follow. In subsequent decades, sapphic humor became an essential part of this battle, particularly in the entertainment industry. During a time when homophobia was thick in the air, comedy served as a pressure valve, breaking down barriers and building bridges to mainstream audiences.

In the 1970s, Robin Tyler became the first out lesbian to appear on television. She wasn't just a comedian—she was a trailblazer. With her sharp wit, Robin showed viewers that Queerness could be funny, relatable, and, most importantly, human. Every laugh she earned was an invitation for people to imagine a world where Queer people could be fully themselves.

And if you were flipping channels back then, you might have stumbled upon Flip Wilson, whose alter ego Geraldine made waves on 1970s variety shows. Geraldine wasn't explicitly

Queer, but Wilson's performance as a sassy, confident woman broke open conversations about gender roles and pushed the boundaries of what mainstream audiences were willing to accept on television. Through laughter, Wilson was creating allyship, inviting viewers into a world where the lines between masculine and feminine, straight and Queer, were deliciously blurred.

Queer comedians didn't just provide laughs—they became mentors for the Queer people watching at home. Public comedy offered a kind of cultural road map. Through these entertainers, LGBTQ+ people were able to see themselves reflected on screen, and they began to understand that joy and humor were not just survival mechanisms—they were tools for building power.

Of course, Ellen DeGeneres made history as the first major sitcom star to come out both in real life and on screen. Her relatable humor and bravery helped bring LGBTQ+ identities into the mainstream. And comedian Margaret Cho became an icon for her unapologetic Queerness. Cho didn't just make people laugh—she made them question what it meant to be an outsider in a society that loves neat little boxes.

And then there's Suzy Eddie Izzard, a comedian who shattered conventions of gender and performance. As Izzard began openly embracing her genderfluid identity, the world didn't turn away—it leaned in. Her years of hilarious and insightful performances helped build a deep connection with fans, allowing comedy to become a way for her to speak about identity in a way audiences could embrace, supporting her journey into a more visible Queer identity.

As many comedians say, "They can't hate you when they're laughing." And that's the power of Queer comedy: It disarms, it connects, and it transforms. Queer comedy didn't just make space for LGBTQ+ people in the entertainment industry; it became a vehicle for broader societal change. These comedians are joyful warriors, using humor to create a more inclusive future—one performance and one burst of laughter at a time.

Joy as a Way Forward

The Queer Community has lived with centuries of trauma inflicted by discriminators, yet we've learned to find joy even in our fight for equity and justice. Fostering joy allows us to maintain peace of mind, survive hardships, and avoid disappearing when times are tough. We don't ignore or dismiss our trauma, but we use joy to support one another through it. Joy is not a scarce resource. Everyone can have moments of joy, especially when it's nurtured by the people around them.

We must look after ourselves before we can shape the world. If you want the world around you to get better, you need to make time to care for yourself first. Joy, laughter, and celebration will fuel you, and we need you at your best for lasting progress to become a reality.

Joy also connects the Queer Community and its allies. Laughter and celebration help us share experiences, building bridges of solidarity. This is why it's so important to welcome allies into joyful Queer spaces—it creates a collective force field that protects everyone from discrimination.

If you really want to unsettle someone who discriminates against you, show them how much fun you're having by being free, bold, and kind. It's a striking contrast: you, glowing with inclusion; them, stuck in bitterness, shaking their fists at people who simply refuse to care about their negativity. Even if spreading joy is the only thing you do to make the world better, it will have a big impact. Happiness is the best argument we have. Everyone is tired of conflict and division; eventually,

We don't ignore or dismiss our trauma, but we use joy to support one another through it.

people gravitate toward the happier crowd and leave the nay-sayers behind.

Be that joyful magnet, and over time, inclusion will win.

IN TODAY'S WORLD, many people feel worn down by constant challenges and conflicts. Triggers will always exist, but joy offers glimmers of hope we need to keep going. Joy gives us a break from the heaviness—allowing us to be real and unguarded without compromise or struggle.

As Queer icon Dan Savage once said: "During the darkest days of the AIDS crisis, we buried our friends in the morning, we protested in the afternoon, and we danced all night. The dance kept us in the fight because it was the dance we were fighting for. It didn't look like we were going to win, and then we did. It doesn't feel like we're going to win, but we could. Keep fighting, keep dancing."

Joy is what truly changes the world. Don't forget to laugh; notice your sources of joy, and immerse yourself in them. It's the best way to get through. Joy is how diversity will win. Now that you're ready to embrace joy, it's important not to wait for others to fail—but that's a lesson for the next chapter!

YOUR RAINBOW WISDOM TOOLKIT

Instead of letting a challenging world get you down, engage these strategies:

- Transform protests into celebrations by organizing joyful, inclusive events that engage and inspire.

- Use humor to disarm prejudice, build bridges, challenge stereotypes, and create understanding across communities.

- In the face of discrimination, turn to the things that make you happy to give you strength.

- Welcome allies into joyful spaces to foster empathy and collective strength.

STOP THE SURVEILLANCE

Respect means accepting that people should live freely, without policing.

They're Watching Us

There's nothing quite as unsettling as being watched. My husband and I learned this on a camel trek in the Sahara, deep in homophobic Morocco, where it's illegal to be gay. We worried our guides might hate or harm us if they realized we were a couple. To stay safe, we hid our relationship. As two usually comfortably out gay men, it felt odd to feel self-conscious. But there we were, caravanning the Sahara, far from cosmopolitan centers and other like-minded tourists, with only the company of kind but suspicious men as our guides.

Deep into the sand dunes, close to the border with Algeria, I kept wondering if the guides we entrusted might turn on us, hate us, or even hurt us if they realized we're gay. The red horizon was mesmerizing, but that couldn't quite distract me from my fear. We both felt vulnerable.

Normally, on a dream vacation, I would be mushy and romantic with my husband. Not this time. I was trying hard to come across as straight out of paranoia and prudence. At night, we slept in our own private bedouin tent. Our mats and blankets had been set up platonically distanced apart. I wanted to pull my mat closer to my husband, but even there, in our own privacy, my guard was up.

Then, the moment I was dreading. I could hear them discussing how the two of us were related. I held my breath. Had they figured us out? Did we act *straight* enough? Was our cover blown? Luckily, after much debate, they concluded we must be distantly related. They figured we knew each other well and took care of each other like family. We couldn't be brothers because we don't look alike, so they decided we must be cousins. Phew, I could relax. I couldn't kiss my husband or hold him as we admired one of the most breathtaking landscapes in the world, but at least I could let my guard down a little.

Although I felt relieved, I resented having to conceal my identity in such a breathtaking place. Queer people—or anyone seen as "different"— shouldn't have to wonder if they are safe just because someone is watching.

Breaking the Panopticon

Imagine a prison where every inmate feels they're being watched at all times, even though they can't always see their guard. This is the essence of the panopticon, a type of institutional architecture conceived by the English philosopher Jeremy Bentham in the late eighteenth century. Bentham describes a circular structure with a central watchtower from which a single guard could observe all prisoners without them knowing whether or not they were being scrutinized. Although it is physically impossible for the single guard to observe all the inmates' cells at once, that the prisoners cannot know when they are being watched motivates them to act as though they are being watched at all times, effectively compelling them to self-regulate.

The concept of the panopticon has found its way into various institutions beyond prisons: schools, hospitals, or anywhere security cameras are set up. In schools, the layout often includes open spaces beside strategically placed administrative offices so that staff can monitor students easily. Hospitals sometimes adopt similar designs to enable nurses and doctors to oversee multiple patients from central hubs. These practices, while intended to enforce rules and promote safety, also create a culture of surveillance. They reinforce the idea that we are always being watched by someone—if not by an authority figure, then by our community—and that we are rewarded when we point out who is not following the "rules."

This motivates us to keep ourselves in check with whatever society deems to be "proper." We police ourselves and others. We then start to shape ourselves and others into being rule followers rather than trusting our own intuition. But this constant surveillance costs people their individuality or authenticity.

You'd think that this type of fear of always being watched and making sure we are staying in line with social norms would be restricted to authoritarian regimes, but this is what many Queer youth experience when they are kept in line by their peers.

A Barrage of Barks

Imagine you're a tween waiting for the school bus, and someone from another group of teenagers barks at you like a dog. You might not think anything of it at first. It's just a harmless bark, right? But then you hear it again while walking down the aisle of the bus, then again down every hallway at school, and then again in every classroom or changeroom, or in the lunchroom. Every single place you go, someone barks at you.

At first, you might be able to convince yourself the barks aren't directed at you, but still, you are haunted by a constant unsettling attack on your confidence wherever you go. You *know* they're barking at you. This social media-driven bullying phenomenon has been plaguing Queer youth all around the world.

To make things worse, most adults, the ones who are supposed to stand up for vulnerable kids, don't do anything about the barking, because the barks are another random noise they hear in their busy day. This is specifically why this form of bullying has become more prevalent. It doesn't get noticed by adults, yet it gets noticed by the target, a Queer youth whose entire existence takes on a soundtrack of confidence-stealing dehumanization.

This is just one type of anti-Queer bullying that some youth face in their day-to-day lives. According to The Trevor Project, the world's leading support network for Queer youth, 2SLGBTQ+ youth are more likely than their straight and cisgender peers to experience bullying through physical, verbal, and electronic forms of harassment. According to their research, almost half of all Queer youth reported intimidation in the past year. And I can tell you from my former life as a teacher, I never met a Queer student who hadn't faced intimidation, exclusion, or mockery.

It can be hard growing up as young Queer person. Not only do they have to navigate a complex world that isn't designed for Queer people, but then there is the harsh realization that their classmates, who are also figuring themselves out, will sometimes experiment with building their confidence at the expense of their Queer classmate. Someday the targeting of Queer people will stop, and yes, in many places it's getting better all the time. But in many places there's still work to be done.

By now it's almost a cliché to talk about the harmful consequences of discrimination on Queer people, but still, it's important to acknowledge how the policing of Queer identities hurts people. According to the Centers for Disease Control and Prevention, this bullying has real-life implications and contributes to higher rates of poor mental health, suicide, and self-harm for Queer people than for the rest of the population. Let's not get stuck there, though; let's become informed and active participants in making the world better for Queer people instead.

Many schools are already supporting and protecting Queer youth by creating education and anti-bullying programs to improve learning and health outcomes. But these efforts don't address a broader issue: Too many young people learn it's acceptable to police others' identities—and then they carry that mindset into adulthood.

So what can we learn from this experience of young Queer people that will make the world a better place? Let's look at some ways to retire our internal prison guard.

Social Norms Hold Us Back

Growing up in a panopticon world convinces us that there is a "right" and "wrong" way to be, and that when people fall out of line, it's our job to tell them. Anyone who has ever been told to come across as "less gay" or "less Queer" knows what I'm talking about. Who made that critic the *boss* anyway? Luckily, no one.

I've already discussed how gender-based social norms restrict us, but their influence extends even further. Think about the expectations we impose on ourselves and others— what defines a healthy relationship, a viable career, or a meaningful pursuit of interests. I've seen entire groups fall into step, collectively mocking those who choose to do things differently. Whether it's criticizing someone's fashion choices, appearance, or approach to relationships, the pattern is the same.

Queer people shouldn't have to wonder if they are safe just because someone is watching.

Policing seeps into how many people approach the whole world. It's a sense of entitlement that many of us carry regarding how others ought to be. Think back to the last gossip session you witnessed or participated in. It's just a big pot of judgment soup, isn't it? We've all done it—sitting with our friends, harping on someone for something like their taste in partners, their new hair color, or how they spend their free time. But it's time we let go of being enforcers.

I believe judgment is warranted when someone causes harm—to themselves, others, the community, or sustainability. But beyond that, we're ready for a world where people are free to explore their identities and life choices without interference. When we finally achieve this, I imagine a collective sigh of relief as the world embraces the freedom to simply be. Imagine that.

It's liberating to realize that no one's identity is *wrong*. We are ready to collectively shift from trusting rigid rules—rules that have cost us all confidence, potential, and the simple joy of existing—to trusting people to be themselves. For many, letting go of control is a challenge. Here are three insightful ways, drawn from leading thinkers, to step back, silence your inner prison guard, and allow others to live freely.

Use Curiosity to Expand Your Perspective

Instead of worrying about how others live their lives, what if you saw their choices as an opportunity to grow? Sociologist Eric Klinenberg emphasizes that embracing diversity strengthens communities and broadens our understanding of the world. When you encounter a choice that feels unfamiliar, reframe it as a chance to learn something new. Try asking someone whom you are tempted to judge or constrain, "What do you love most about this?" *or* "How has this shaped your life?" Viewing people's experiences as a window into different ways of living turns curiosity into self-expansion. You don't have to agree—you just have to be open. Who knows? You might even find inspiration for your own journey.

Strengthen Relationships with Active Listening

Stepping out of the control zone begins with empathy—not just understanding someone's choices but making them feel truly heard. Psychologist Carl Rogers found that practicing active listening fosters trust and deepens relationships. The next time someone shares something you don't relate to, resist the urge to critique. Instead, ask, "What led you to this decision?" Then reflect their words back with, "It sounds like this really matters to you because…" This practice builds meaningful bonds, making others feel valued and seen. Rogers's person-centered approach doesn't just help them—it strengthens your ability to connect on a deeper level.

Step Back to Allow for Growth

Letting go of control isn't about giving up—it's about stepping back and allowing growth. Author, speaker, and researcher Brené Brown has shown us that trust builds stronger relationships and thrives on vulnerability. Instead of micromanaging, practice trust in action. Say, "I know you've got this—let me know how I can support you." When someone takes a risk and it doesn't work out, be the person who asks, "What did you learn?" instead of saying "I told you so." Trust isn't passive—it's an active choice to let go, create space for others to step up, and free yourself from the burden of control.

LET'S FOCUS ON fostering a culture that respects and supports people living true to themselves. We need to break the culture of surveillance and foster a culture of trusting people to be themselves. The beautiful part of this lesson is that as soon as you start letting other people be themselves, you're freer to stop policing yourself too.

Live Like No One Is Watching

We all know the saying, "Dance like no one is watching." But this cliché holds so much truth: Be free, because no one else really cares. And if they do care, ignore them.

If you struggle with knowing what you want, or you are the type of person who looks mostly to others for guidance on how to be, this could be a sign that your intuition and self-resolve have been knocked out of you through a life of being overly observed or criticized. A good mental pathway to combat self-doubt or indecision is to lean on your values. In a moment of indecision or doubt, remind yourself what is important to *you*. What do you really care about?

There's a lot of power in living this way. As people age, many of them speak about a time in their life when they finally found freedom and joy, when they stopped caring what others think. The truth is, people are always going to watch us, but if we can unshackle ourselves from that gaze, render it powerless, then we are free to live how we know we are supposed to be. We can live free from irrelevant outside pressures and truthfully for ourselves. Go ahead, try it—live like no one is watching.

OUR WORLD has conditioned us to police ourselves and others, often without realizing it. Many people live as if they're constantly waiting for others to step out of line, ready to critique them for being different or making unconventional choices. But we can shift this mindset. Instead of reinforcing surveillance, let's embrace freedom and trust—for both ourselves and others. In the next chapter I'll go deeper into more ways to feel comfortable being fully you.

YOUR RAINBOW WISDOM TOOLKIT

Breaking the culture of surveillance starts with small, intentional actions. The more we let people be themselves, the freer we become too.

- Let go of "way-of-life" enforcement and recognize that everyone deserves the freedom to be themselves.

- Shift from criticizing differences to being curious. Invite people to share their perspective before forming an opinion.

- Instead of jumping to judgment, practice active listening to build trust and understanding with others.

- Step back and allow people to navigate their own choices. Support growth rather than anticipating failure.

- Rely on your values—not external approval—to guide you, and enjoy the freedom that comes from not policing yourself or others.

LGBTQ+ LIFE LESSON #10

COME OUT AS YOURSELF

Queer people show us
the power of sharing our
true self with the world.

The Wedding Ring Dilemma

Since I wear a wedding ring, people often ask about my wife. In that moment, I have a choice. Do I evade the subject completely? Do I correct them and mention my husband? Or do I just vaguely refer to my partner, because I have a gut feeling that mentioning him would probably lead to me facing discrimination?

I've made each of these choices at different times.

When I was pulled over for a speeding ticket, and the police officer asked me personal questions, I decided to be honest and got the maximum fine. Would it have turned out differently if I had lied and talked about my wife? I'll never know.

I once avoided correcting a coworker who assumed I was married to a woman. Whenever the subject came up, I would mention "my partner." But over the months we spent working together, things got so awkward that I had to come out. From then on, our relationship felt strained. Was it because I wasn't honest from the get-go? Or was it because my intuition about their homophobia was spot-on? I'll never know.

When my husband and I first moved into our neighborhood of mostly elderly straight people, lots of them asked if my husband was my son! I mean, he definitely looks younger than me (we're five years apart in age), but not twenty years younger! Geez, not only did that make me consider a Botox appointment right away, but I had to wonder why that was the most logical conclusion they could come up with. Talk about awkward conversations. I had to come out in those first moments of meeting them and tell them we are happily married, and many of them appeared embarrassed for asking.

Coming Out Is a Constant Decision

In a world that casually assumes everyone is straight or cisgender, Queer people constantly face the choice of whether to come out. We already know we are Queer—coming out is more about breaking others' assumptions. And whenever you challenge someone's thinking like that, you never know how they're going to react.

In places where Queer people are safe and accepted, or if someone already feels confident, coming out can feel like no big deal. But when safety isn't guaranteed, Queer people must do a quick mental calculation: If I share my true identity, will I be safe? Will there be any fallout? Am I about to deal with drama? Will I be treated differently? The constant risk assessment is exhausting.

When I talk about coming out with straight people, some will say, "That's your private business. No one should need a label." But no one tells a straight wife that having a husband is their "private business." This double standard pushes Queer people into the closet.

You'd be surprised how many times I am casually asked things that require me to mention my personal life. I remember my first few job interviews as a budding marketing executive in downtown Toronto. Of course, no one explicitly asked if I was gay, but at some point I always faced a crossroads. Should I be fully authentic? Or should I keep things vague and risk coming across as uninterested or, worse, a liar? If I didn't get the job, of course I wondered whether it had anything to do with my sexuality. If I did get the job, how and when would I come out, and how would that go?

Even in some of the most progressive and inclusive countries in the world, up to 40 percent of Queer people stay closeted at work. That means four out of ten Queer people are afraid or hesitant to be fully transparent at work, and that drains energy that could be spent on their creativity and success. Many Queer people still fear their career trajectory will be affected should they share their true identity. Queer people don't always feel safe or want to attract drama from those who just don't get it.

Workplace diversity inclusion expert Michael Bach calls this the *Curse of Constantly Coming Out.* He describes how the relentless cycle that LGBTQ+ individuals face in repeatedly disclosing their identity creates a perpetual state of vulnerability and stress in them. As Queer individuals navigate environments that may not always be supportive, this stressful cycle of constant risky disclosure often leads to decreased job satisfaction and lower productivity. At its best, this cycle can be a disheartening experience. At its worst, it can exact a terrible toll on a Queer person's mental health and overall well-being.

Most employers and leaders should shudder at the thought of their employees not feeling safe, because it leaves them unable to contribute fully. In the mid-2010s, Google's Project Aristotle found that psychological safety was the most crucial factor in team success. Teams where members felt comfortable taking risks and being open with each other were more innovative, productive, and successful overall.

A notable example of fostering psychological safety around employees' identities is Rolls-Royce's "Being Like Me" initiative. Launched in 2022, this program encourages employees to share personal stories on the company's intranet, promoting understanding and reducing the need for individuals to conceal aspects of their identity at work: By creating a platform where employees feel safe to express their true self, Rolls-Royce has embedded inclusion and belonging into its organizational culture. I hope I get to see a dashing Rolls-Royce in a Pride parade someday!

When we are on guard, our brain can't perform the same way it would with a sense of sustained security. The world would be so much better if there wasn't so much effort being put into protecting ourselves and constant mental calculations of safety.

What Is Code-Switching?

The opposite of coming out is *code-switching*—adjusting how we present ourselves to fit in with dominant groups and social norms. The term originated in reference to spoken language: Code-switching is the practice of alternating between two or more languages, dialects, or ways of speaking depending on the social context. This phenomenon often occurs when individuals feel the need to conform to the expectations of different social groups to gain acceptance or avoid discrimination. Anyone who comes from a community with a prominent accent or dialect has probably experienced the pressure to code-switch.

For example, I'm always amazed how my friends from Newfoundland can switch between their local dialect to a more formal English. They've told me they drop their accent to fit in or avoid harmful stereotypes. I think the accent sounds authentic and beautiful, but I understand some Newfoundlanders feel the pressure to sound like everyone else in certain situations.

Some of my Indigenous friends have also had to change how they speak around non-Indigenous people to avoid racist assumptions about their education or status. It embarrasses me now when I recall myself as a teacher correcting my Indigenous students for saying "seen" instead of "saw." I realize now that every time I corrected them, I was pressuring them to code-switch. I was pushing them to hide their background to sound more formal, essentially making them suppress their identity. I pushed colonial English onto them and made them feel as though they had to speak a certain way to get good grades or acceptance from teachers—and, by extension, from other white people.

In many ways, code-switching is akin to a survival strategy. For example, a Black professional might speak in African American Vernacular English with friends and family but switch to Standard American English in a corporate meeting. This switch isn't just about language; it's about navigating social landscapes and managing perceptions. If we extend the concept of code-switching more broadly, we can see that marginalized individuals have to do this all the time: They change or hide aspects of themselves to blend in, fit in, or succeed in a world that is often controlled by folks with differences from them.

Here are some other examples of how people might code-switch their identity:

- dressing one way for work but differently in personal life

- altering hairstyles, makeup, or grooming to fit professional or societal standards

- using a more common name instead of a culturally specific one

- downplaying religious or cultural identity in secular spaces

- hiding disabilities, chronic illnesses, or mental health struggles

- modifying social media presence to project success or conformity

- choosing a career for respectability rather than passion

- adjusting relationship dynamics to meet societal expectations

- avoiding personal anecdotes or traditions that might seem "different"

Although code-switching can be a valuable skill, allowing for smooth navigation across diverse social settings, it carries significant emotional cost. Code-switching is a continuous mental adjustment that, over time, can hinder genuine self-expression in anyone.

Belonging and Fitting In Are Worlds Apart

"Fitting in" means evaluating a group of people and thinking, "Who do I need to be? What do I need to wear? How should I act? What should I say?" to succeed. It means changing who you are to match the expectations of others. But true belonging allows you to be yourself and be accepted for that.

For many marginalized people, the choice is often stark: Blend in or leave. After years of building a celebrated and successful teaching career, I found myself face-to-face with a boss who embodied exclusionary attitudes. Based on the hate that flashed across her eyes when I first met her, her ongoing sneers, and how she stood in my way at every opportunity, I had an instinct her behavior was rooted in homophobia.

I realized that staying would mean compromising who I was. For me, leaving became the only option.

Luckily, I had alternatives. I was ready to launch an exciting career as an LGBTQ+ inclusion speaker, trainer, and strategist. But I know not everyone has the same privileges or options. My career-ending boss didn't just undermine me; she effectively set up a roadblock on the professional path I had spent years building. That is the power of exclusion: It doesn't just push people out; it can strip them of dreams they've worked a lifetime to achieve.

Trying to fit in takes an immense toll. Alan Turing, the brilliant mathematician and father of modern computing, illustrated the deep loneliness that comes from hiding one's true self. Despite his groundbreaking work cracking the Enigma code—helping to end World War II sooner—he lived in a society that criminalized his identity as a gay man.

To the world, he was a visionary; in private, he bore the crushing weight of secrecy. In 1952, the very government he had helped save convicted him of "gross indecency," sentencing him to chemical castration. The humiliation and persecution took their toll, and in 1954, at just forty-one, Turing died from cyanide poisoning, a tragic event widely believed to be suicide.

Turing's story demonstrates the devastating impact of living a life that denies authenticity. The toll of hiding his true self and the persecution he faced for being who he was led to a tragic and untimely end—an irreparable loss to both humanity and the fields of technology and science.

It takes guts to be yourself, and the more you do it, the more others will too. Everyone can model authenticity by sharing their vulnerabilities, ideas, and curiosities. How many times have you wanted to say something but you thought others would think it's stupid, so you limited yourself?

To counter self-doubt, try imposing less pressure on yourself. We can all make gains by considering our ideas less as absolutes and more as building blocks for others to riff on. Your idea doesn't have to be correct or the be-all-end-all to be valuable; no idea is a full solution, but rather part of getting toward one. Think of ideas as steps to a final goal rather than the destination. This creates a community of collaboration and idea sharing rather than hierarchy.

Good ideas rarely come from trying to be the same as everyone else or repeating how things have always been done. We need to hear new things and see things in new ways to move society forward. Think about how much richer and more vibrant our communities could be if we all showed up as our true selves, ready to share ideas that help move people closer to their goals, and if we lived in a society where our differences were celebrated, not masked. Our connections would be stronger, our solutions more robust and detailed, our interactions more genuine, and our lives more fulfilling.

Four Ways to Show Up as You

Authenticity serves us all, so let's look at four ways we can all show up as ourselves more, for everyone's benefit.

Practice Self-Affirmation

To show up as your authentic self in every space, practice self-affirmation, which involves reminding yourself of your strengths and worth. Use self-talk like, "They are lucky to have me here," "I am enough as I am," or "My uniqueness is my strength." Engaging in self-empowerment can help you stay grounded in your true self. Confidence in who you are reduces the tendency to conform to external pressures.

It takes guts
to be yourself.
The more you
do it, the more
others will too.

Get Comfortable with Being Vulnerable

So often, people feel as if they have to be perfect to succeed, but the power of vulnerability teaches us that we can embrace and share failures in order to succeed. I call it *lose to win.* When I use vulnerability in my high-stakes speeches, the crowd responds so much better after I have revealed some of my struggle or rough edges to them. All of a sudden, they are rooting for me rather than being skeptical.

Remember You Are a Gift

People remember those who make the world their own and re-create it using their own personal outlook. So, practice contributing what you have to offer and standing bravely as yourself. Believing that you were born to be you, and no one else, can be a powerful mantra. In moments of insecurity, tell yourself, "The best gift I can give the world is to be myself."

Challenge Conformity

To challenge conformity, the best route is to name it in yourself and in others. Are you saying something because you think someone wants you to or because you actually believe it? Of course, you want the answer to be that you are saying it because you believe it wholeheartedly. Believe, believe! By doing so, you pave the way for everyone to do the right thing, not the common thing. Be the change, be yourself, and then you will truly belong.

Come Out as Yourself

In the search for self-fulfillment and self-actualization, many Queer people have had to learn the courage and the value of coming out instead of code-switching. By embracing who we are, instead of who society wants us to be, we are fulfilling what we were born to do. Queer or not, you can conquer your fear of not fitting in.

If you feel drained after being with certain people, this can be a good clue you are code-switching around them. If they can't handle the real you, they weren't friends with *you*—they were friends with a version of you that you had to create for them. And if you're holding back the true person you are, you are not being the friend, lover, leader, coworker, or artist you are destined to be. Grow into your gifts, not the gifts of others.

Many Queer people grew up in a world where standing out was shamed out of them, and so they hid their differences under heavy armor. Even if you're not Queer, you can take off the armor that no longer serves you. It's not protecting you; it's dragging you down, keeping you from being truly known as the person you really are—so come out as yourself!

Now that you're on board with embracing your true self, let's talk ourselves out of thinking we have to fix ourselves to be better, in LGBTQ+ Life Lesson #11.

YOUR RAINBOW WISDOM TOOLKIT

We all feel pressure to code-switch at times, but the cost of it is wasted energy and hindered potential. To nurture authenticity:

- notice when you're hiding or downplaying who you are—it drains energy you could be using for genuine connections and creativity;

- practice self-talk like "I am enough" or "They're lucky to have me here" to ground yourself in your own worth;

- share your struggles, missteps, or quirks—vulnerability fosters deeper trust and belonging;

- ask whether you're going along with the crowd just to fit in—push back by offering your true ideas, style, and voice; and

- when someone else shows up as their authentic self, encourage and applaud them, creating a ripple of acceptance around you.

YOU DON'T NEED TO BE FIXED

Queer people aren't broken and don't need fixing—and neither does anyone else.

Shooting Stars

Growing up in a small rural town where anything unusual was a target for bullies, excelling became my shield. In high school, the honor roll rankings were posted every term, and I'd run feverishly to check them. If I wasn't ranked first, I was crushed. Luckily, most of the time, I was. I'm not telling this to brag but to show how deeply I needed to excel. It wasn't just about achievement—it felt like survival. If I wasn't the "smartest," I feared I'd be known for something far more dangerous: being different.

Looking back, I realize I used my academic standing as a way to deflect negative attention. My mindset boiled down to this: "If I stand out for being the best at school, maybe they'll stop calling me a fag."

It wasn't just about escaping bullying—it was about escaping altogether. Deep down, I knew that to find myself, I had to get out of my small town. I remember telling myself, "I have to win a scholarship if I want to get out of this place." My caring single mom couldn't afford to send me away, so I knew it was all on me. I had to be a shooting star to escape my homophobic universe. At the time, I wasn't even out. I didn't fully understand I was gay, though I had crushes on boys that I explained away in other terms.

My drive didn't stop at grades. I got involved in community leadership and local initiatives. If I couldn't help myself, maybe I could help others. It felt like a way to look outward, rather than turning inward to confront my own truths. And it worked: I earned a fully funded ride out of town and never looked back. Excelling became my escape route, and through it, I found freedom and, eventually, self-confidence.

At university, everything changed. I built self-worth through community. Then, with my degree in hand, I moved to downtown Toronto, Canada's economic and cultural hub, which was eye-opening. Successful gay people seemed to be everywhere—politicians, innovators, and creators shaping marketing, fashion, and culture. Later, in Vancouver, I saw it again: Queer people blazing trails and breaking barriers.

It made me wonder: Does being Queer make people exceptional? Is there something about being different that helps Queer people see possibilities others can't? Maybe you've noticed it too—a dazzling number of LGBTQ+ people leading in art, tech, activism, and beyond.

But the truth is more complex. Many Queer people are overachievers—not just out of ambition but because of the challenges of being part of a minority. For many, the world sends them an unspoken message: "You have to prove yourself."

Overachievement as a Survival Strategy

The idea that many Queer people are overachievers is supported by research. A study by John Pachankis in *Basic and Applied Social Psychology* found that sexual minority men put more energy into achievement than their straight peers. They pursued more education, earned higher grades, and were more involved in community organizations; they even put more effort into their outward appearance. Pachankis explains this as a way for Queer people to gain recognition as a means to safety. Success can feel like an escape from stigma—a way to belong.

Of course, not every Queer person is an overachiever. My husband put it perfectly. He once said, "How many out gay construction workers or plumbers do you know? Those weren't even options for me. That world would've been too cruel." Without top grades in high school, he felt that as a gay guy his options were limited to careers like hairstyling, nursing, or customer service. He built a successful career in his own right, but the idea that he ever felt his options were constrained by a double whammy of not feeling like an overachiever in his younger days along with the exclusion of others is uncomfortable to me.

For all its rewards, overachievement comes with costs. Overachievement as a survival strategy can take a toll. The Pachankis study found that though Queer people are more likely to pursue outward success, the pressure can lead to negative self-image, isolation, and emotional distress. It's like running a marathon with no finish line; the relentless need to prove yourself can be exhausting and unsustainable.

Yet there's incredible resilience in Queer people. Many Queer individuals turn discrimination into strength. The coping skills they develop help them succeed in other areas of life. But it's a double-edged sword. While those skills open doors, the constant need to prove one's worth is a heavy burden.

Still, Queer resilience is remarkable. Turning adversity into motivation and thriving in spaces not designed for you is no small feat. But maybe the ultimate win for Queer overachievers isn't personal success—it's a world where they no longer have to prove their worth to anyone.

Queer people are a gift to the world, but that doesn't mean they should be burdened with a need to prove it. They don't need to be fixed, and they don't want to be. No one should ever have to feel as if they're broken just for existing, yet the world around us can't stop trying to fix us anyway.

When You Fix Something, You Break Something Else

Whether it's an influencer or a multilevel marketing company peddling some cure, contraption, or concept, we are constantly being asked to spend hard-earned cash on a never-ending conveyor belt of new ways to fix ourselves. However you show up in the algorithm, someone has figured out a way to target you with something you *absolutely* must have.

Maybe it's a life coach who has a formula for you to finally achieve a goal, a beverage that will make you feel better, cosmetics that minimize wrinkles, or an app that will improve your sleep, memory, or stress levels. I'm not saying there aren't things out there that can help us, but I'm also sure all those things won't make your life that much better. And most of them will end up in a landfill.

Advertisers and sellers prey on our insecurities with hopes of cashing in on them. I should know—my undergrad degree is in marketing, and I spent a few years working for the world's largest consumer packaged goods company and then on advertising campaigns for some of North America's biggest brands. I even did market research that involved going into the homes of housewives to observe their daily housekeeping chores in search of yet another solution to make their lives "better." That's Marketing 101: Identify a potential need, frame it as a problem that needs to be solved, and then sell them the solution.

However, the problem is that a lot of this activity around making ourselves "better" actually makes our lives worse;

the planet and climate are clearly suffering from our over-consumption. But it gets even more personal than that. We've all seen the media reports showing that unreasonable beauty standards affect the self-esteem and mental health of every-one. And then there's all the extra work and time we have to put in to afford all this stuff, at the expense of our free time, health, nutritious food, and proven self-care methods like exercise, human connection, or time in nature.

You have to ask yourself: What are we really fixing, and how much of us is truly broken? Thankfully, there are shifts revealing a new way to be for us all.

Shifting Standards

At its best, our society develops language of encouragement—a way of flipping things that were once seen as flaws into sources of pride. Take the rise of appreciation for "dad bods" and "short kings." These terms, once used to diminish, are now badges of honor.

The "dad bod" celebrates a physique that's neither overly lean nor heavily muscled. It reflects a balanced lifestyle, where indulgence and self-care coexist. Celebrities like comedian Ian Harvie, actor Leonardo DiCaprio (who doesn't even have kids), and musician Drake have helped normal-ize this body type, proving that attractiveness isn't limited to those with extremely low body fat. The dad bod is a symbol of relatability, self-acceptance, and redefining masculinity on one's own terms.

Similarly, the term "short king" celebrates men of shorter stature, highlighting their charisma, confidence, and contri-butions rather than focusing on their height. Think of actors like Elliot Page, Leo Sheng, and Jeremy Allen White. For too long, shorter men have faced societal biases that linked height to value or strength. The "short king" movement proves that physical dimensions don't define one's worth, presence, or appeal.

In the feminine sphere, change is also happening. Historically, being petite or thin has often been upheld as the gold standard of beauty, but that's shifting. Today, thick body types and booty-forward aesthetics are front and center, as people embrace a broader spectrum of beauty. Beauty icon Pamela Anderson has gained recognition for embracing life without makeup, showing that authenticity can be just as beautiful as—if not more than—the curated perfection often portrayed in media. It's clear that preferred body shapes and appearances will always shift across time and culture, so we might as well accept all the different versions of human as beautiful right now.

These shifting standards challenge the idea that we must constantly enhance or alter ourselves to be considered beautiful, focusing instead on self-love and natural confidence. These conversations remind us that everyone deserves to feel celebrated. And these are the kinds of movements we need to change how we see each other, but also how we see ourselves.

We can all take part in recognizing and celebrating our own individuality and diversity. It's so tempting to think we aren't good enough, but you can find your true power when you lean into your unique strengths and transform negative perceptions into positive, empowering narratives about yourself.

Here are some examples of talking about your attributes as strengths and celebrating them, rather than thinking you are broken:

1   Body positivity: This movement embraces curves and plus-sized bodies, and all types of bodies for that matter.

2 Nerd culture and geek chic: Being a nerd or geek has been reframed as cool, desirable, exciting, and creative. Think of the boom in cosplay conventions, comic book–inspired movies, and normcore fashion.

3 Mental health awareness: Once taboo, talking openly about mental health struggles and strategies is now mainstream.

4 Independence and singlehood: Many used to view singlehood as a weakness, but a new narrative reframes being single as a period of self-discovery and a liberating experience.

5 Aging gracefully: Getting older is a gift and can be a time of empowerment and wisdom.

Being Queer Is About Self-Acceptance

For much of my early life, I thought I was broken because I wasn't straight. And the world around me tried to convince me that attributes other than my own were better. But I wasn't broken—I know that now. Maybe at some point in your life you've thought and felt the same. But guess what—you aren't broken either!

The Queer Community is all about embracing who you are. Full stop. Furry and husky bears are some of the most close-knit people and best party throwers in the gay community. Butch dykes lean into their masculinity, grit, and roughness as an advantage. Pansexuals aren't limited by gender when it comes to attraction. Trans people know their true gender even in a world that has labeled them something else from their first moments on earth. Intersex people understand that their anatomy or chromosomes are more than what people assume they are.

The truth is that your uniqueness is what makes you special. It's time to unleash ourselves from a world that tells us we don't fit in, and shift into a perspective that who we are is good enough. Comparing yourself to others might be part of what's holding you back.

Are You Addicted to Ranking Yourself?

Our society encourages us to rank ourselves by certain ideals—being the toughest, most rugged, strongest, fastest, handiest, prettiest, most caring, most hospitable, manliest, or most feminine. All these statements really do is burden us with pressure to be the *most*. But since very few people get to be the *most*, the rest of us are left feeling like we're not good enough. So much so that so many of us spend much of our free time and disposable cash trying to become something we're not.

I'm not saying that setting goals for yourself is wrong, but your goals don't always have to be about being "better." This "I'm not good enough" thinking drags people down. One way this shows up in our lives is through resolutions—New Year's resolutions, dieting culture, and other inadequacy-based thinking. These goals come from a place of thinking we aren't good enough—and Queer people are weighed down with this feeling too often.

What if you set goals from the perspective of honoring who you really are or who you feel you are destined to be? Now, instead of *fixing* yourself, you're leaning into *becoming* yourself. Who you are is good enough. What an inspiration!

Instead of fixing yourself, lean into who you are.

Antidotes to "Self-Improvement"

Life is about fulfillment, not just self-improvement. Here is some language that might help you find out who you are rather than try to fix yourself. Give it a shot, grab a piece of paper and a pen, and finish these sentences. Try to be as specific as you can.

- I'm the most "me" when _______________.

- I still want to learn _______________.

- I still want to try _______________.

- I'm the most confident when _______________.

- My dream is to _______________.

- I feel most alive and energized when I _______________.

- The people who make me feel the best about myself are _______________.

- I can be kinder to myself about _______________.

- I feel good when I express my _______________.

- I want to make more time for _______________.

- The best parts of me come out when _______________.

- Something I still want to learn about myself is _______________.

- A moment I hope will flash before my eyes when I die is _______________.

All your answers are clues to things that might make your life more fulfilling. Don't feel pressured by them, though. That's not the point of this exercise! It's about noticing those things that add to your life and then leaning into them, rather than always trying to fix the things society pressures us about.

WE'VE ALL only got one shot. Your life is yours to live, so you might as well love it. Do the things that fulfill you, not others. If something is standing in your way, then maybe that thing is the problem, not you. When you accept yourself for exactly who you are, rather than always trying to fix yourself, you might realize that those moments that you've been denying yourself are truly worth your attention.

Instead of thinking you still have to become something to be a good version of yourself, or thinking that you have yet to achieve something, try leaning into the parts of you that should be expanded and nurtured. Those are your guideposts to fulfillment. And when your heart lights up, that's a sign something is worth experiencing. And that kind of spark is exactly what I'm going to talk about in the next LGBTQ+ Life Lesson.

YOUR RAINBOW WISDOM TOOLKIT

Here are some ways you can learn to be yourself, rather than other people's idea of "better":

- Challenge the "fix-me" myth. Call out language that pressures people to prove or fix themselves.

- Focus on and amplify your worth over relentless achievement.

- Disrupt perfectionism by leaning into what fulfills you, and own it.

- Swap judgmental, self-improvement talk with affirmations of being good enough.

- Take concrete steps to create environments where Queer lives are truly valued.

LEAN INTO YOUR GATEWAY EMOTIONS

A gateway emotion
is the spark of
excitement that reveals
the life you can have
when you trust it.

Should've, Could've, Would've

I'm not someone who has many regrets, but the few I do have stem from the times I denied my gateway emotions. As a child, I loved giving dance performances because I felt so free and special, but after one public school performance where I was teased mercilessly—even by adults—I stopped dancing. The ridicule didn't just take away my love of dancing; it took away my gateway emotion. They beat out of me something I cherished so deeply—a spark that deserved to be fanned, not stomped out.

Looking back, I wish I had leaned into that escape from my often lonely childhood and embraced that inner light—something that shone brighter than almost anything else. Instead, it was taken from me. Even now, thirty-five years later, whenever I see a male ballet dancer, I think, *That could have been me.*

It's not just regret over missing a world filled with beautiful, flexible men (though, let's be honest, there's that too!). It's a deeper sense that my journey to accepting myself as a gay, Queer man might have been smoother in that world. I would have found confidence so much earlier, and who knows what else about myself as a result?

People tell me it's not too late to learn ballet, but it's not about the dance moves. It's the personal development I missed out on—that version of myself I know I could have discovered. Not being a ballet dancer is my one true regret, because it meant missing the chance to fully know myself in this lifetime. And I can never get that back.

Embracing the Spark

The first moment a little Queer boy or a young trans feminine person tries on makeup, Mom's high heels, or maybe a wig or dress, something magical happens—it's as if a light switches on in their soul. Talk to any Queer person and you'll hear how a small, simple act can unlock a deep sense of joy and comfort in their own skin.

This experience is like a moment of temporary time travel when someone gets to feel the promise of their own future. Within that moment of a gateway emotion, a confidence wells up inside, which will someday come to the surface when that person is ready to embrace who they are inside. It's as if Queer spirits know that someday they will fully find themselves despite the stigma and social norms around them.

For young lesbians, Queer people, and trans masculine folks, the same feeling can arise the first time they pack (wear a stuffed sock or something phallic under their clothes), try on "boys'" underwear, or bind their chest. I've seen this same joy when cis-straight guys try drag for the first time— suddenly, a playful version of themselves can come out, free from "bro-pressure" and shame. These gateway emotions lead to feeling fully alive as yourself. Everyone deserves a chance to shine and be free, Queer or not. Busting out of "normal" is liberating for anyone, and it doesn't have to be tied to identity.

People trapped in the panopticon (LGBTQ+ Life Lesson #9) often miss these gateway moments because they pour so much energy into fitting in that they never find their way into authenticity. This is why removing the pressure of surveillance is vital, because it frees people to discover who they really are.

You owe it to yourself to notice when life gives you those hints that you are finally being true to yourself, whether it be a sense of ease or of elation washing over your body. Notice those moments, cherish them, and see what they teach you. Those gateway emotions open the door to your authentic self. Trust that spark of intuition showing you your destiny. It takes courage, but you deserve to embrace your gateway emotion for the rest of your life.

A gateway emotion doesn't have to be a *big* thing. It can be as simple as a new relationship, hobby, adventure or idea. The beauty lies in recognizing it within yourself. Sometimes people label these "gateway" interests as problematic and steer us away from our natural, intuitive passions. But imagine if more of us leaned into the temptation to be free and authentic, rather than turning away from it. Queer people shining brightly remind us all to let our inner light show and step toward our gateway emotions. Yet there's a powerful emotion that can block us from stepping fully into these possibilities: shame.

Shame May Stand in Your Way

To me, there's nothing more beautiful than a field of flowers dotting the landscape. My favorite view is a field of poppies in Provence or a rainbow of Alpine meadows close to a mountain's summit. As a kid, I had that same sense of wonder, obsessively taking pictures of every flower, while my mom hurried me along.

But I remember the moment I started hiding my love of flowers. I felt ashamed because nobody else seemed excited when I showed them my pictures, and I kept hearing, "That's not what boys like." So I stopped noticing and celebrating them.

Shame is tricky—it's often a mix of influences from people we admire, events in our lives, and outside forces like the media. Regardless of where shame comes from, it affects our confidence, abilities, interests, and, hauntingly, our self-perception. Still, although we may not be able to control its origins, we can decide to stop continuing to shame ourselves.

When you notice a gateway emotion—a spark of potential, goodness, love, or curiosity—you're feeling the opposite of shame. Shame might try to sneak back in, but that shame isn't you. Instead, lean into the gateway emotion. The more you flex that muscle of confidence rather than magnifying shame, the more you'll be able to let it go and embrace your authentic self. It takes practice. By trusting your gateway emotion instead of shame, you strengthen the bridge between your confidence and your true desires. When you honor what genuinely matters to you, rather than what you think others expect, you build your own moral authority.

Moral authority is conviction in yourself—a deep knowing of who you are. It is a confidence in what is important to you and it is one of the key components of self-confidence. You are your own boss! And when you fully believe you have the right to be your own boss, you weaken the force of the shame imposed on you by others.

Honor Your Intuition

Research supports the idea that trusting and engaging with gut feelings leads to greater happiness. People who trust their intuition often experience more positive emotional outcomes. A study published in *Frontiers in Psychology* examined

Get to know yourself fully in this lifetime.

how people feel after making intuitive choices compared with more analytical ones. The study found that individuals who followed their gut experienced intensified positive emotions after a successful outcome compared with those who relied on logic or analysis. The study implies that we will all make mistakes, but those of us who follow intuition will end up happier.

There's also research suggesting that following intuition can lead to success, particularly in high-stakes fields like finance and leadership. For instance, a study of financial traders showed that those who were more attuned to their bodily signals (such as a quickened pulse and tightening muscles) achieved better results. This ability to rely on somatic markers—physical cues from the body—resulted in faster, more accurate decision-making, demonstrating that intuition, when tuned properly, can be a powerful asset in achieving success.

These findings suggest that developing intuitive awareness, whether through bodily signals or emotional insights, can contribute to better outcomes in both personal and professional settings. Essentially, it's about trusting yourself rather than the world around you to know what's right. If you're hoping for more convincing, take a cue from the Queer Community; they teach us all how to be the authentic versions of ourselves.

Many of the Queer people who shine brightest live fully and authentically, ignoring the pressures to be what others want. They honor their gateway emotions and lean into who they truly are.

Still, I know some of you may not have the freedom to live out loud due to discrimination. That doesn't mean those who are closeted can't let their light shine—indeed, they need the joy of honoring their gateway emotions more than anyone.

If you do have the privilege, safety, and security to lean into your gateway emotions—whether they involve a Queer aspect of your identity or something else—trust what your heart shows you. As long as it doesn't harm others or yourself through violence, abuse, or lack of consent, you owe it to yourself to honor that gateway emotion.

WE ALL have those moments in life where we get hints about who we truly are and what it means to be alive. Only you can know what those moments have been. If you have trouble noticing them, search for those electric, buzzing, clear, sharp, and exhilarating moments in your past. You will never regret being true to yourself. Even if you face obstacles, at least you'll meet them as your most authentic self rather than as an impostor.

In the next chapter, we'll talk about the importance of breaking the rules that might still be holding you back.

YOUR RAINBOW WISDOM TOOLKIT

Here's how to step into those gateway emotions and discover a more beautiful life on the other side:

- Pay attention to those electric moments—your "gateway emotions"—that hint at who you truly are.

- Let go of the voices telling you you're wrong; honor the joy and curiosity that guide you.

- Following your intuition can boost both your happiness and your success. Embrace what feels authentically you.

- When you strengthen your self-belief by deciding what matters to you, rather than letting others define your worth, you build your own moral authority.

BREAK YOUR CORNERSTONE RULES

Queer people
inspire us to break
cornerstone rules
that no longer suit us.

He Wears Long Shorts

I was once on holiday in Mexico with a group of people I barely knew. One of them was Fred, who was quiet and conservative—more at home in a hardware store than on a beach in small-town Mexico. He was the kind of guy who made blunt political statements and had firm ideas about the world. But the thing that surprised me was that he always wore heavy denim or thick corduroy pants, even in the blazing heat on the beach.

After a few days, I couldn't help but ask why he never wore shorts. He shrugged and said, "It's just a rule I have. Grew up on a farm, always wore pants, so I still wear pants." I understood that this makes sense when you are working around heavy machinery and animals. This clothing habit didn't seem like self-consciousness—just a protective rule he'd stuck to. I, on the other hand, have mostly been a rule-bender for most of my life. So, being my ever-encouraging self, I started encouraging Fred to get *wild* and wear shorts.

Now, this is where I should pause to make a comment about convincing people to do things. We should never try to convince people to do things that make them feel unsafe or compromise their values. But in this case, Fred was stuck in a childhood rule that he had never thought to question, until someone asked him.

Much to my surprise, Fred finally showed up on the beach in board shorts. The funny thing is, they were the longest board shorts you could find, and they might as well have been pants—but not to him! He had broken his cornerstone rule and, with a huge smile on his face, he told me that he felt great!

Fred's decision to swap denim for board shorts may look like a small style choice on the surface, but it speaks to a powerful shift underneath: the willingness to question and break self-imposed limitations.

Take Off Your Pants!

We all have a pair of pants we're afraid to take off—invisible fences we build around our lives. These are the cornerstone rules we create to keep us "safe" from some assumed failure, embarrassment, or discomfort. Instead of seeing these rules as a protective barrier, consider them for what they truly are: limits on what you can accomplish and what you might find comfort or joy in.

But what if, just once, you threw out the rule book, ripped off those pants, and said, "I'll give this a shot!" Whether it's speaking up when you normally wouldn't, trying an outfit that feels bold, talking to that person you wouldn't talk to usually, or being *you* in a new way, the key to breaking your own rules is to stop assuming the worst and start giving yourself the chance to be amazed. Besides, you can always put those long pants right back on! But perhaps don't be so quick to do so.

Change doesn't always feel magical in the moment. It can feel strange, awkward, and even downright uncomfortable at first. That's okay. Be patient with yourself. Learning to live outside your self-imposed limits takes practice. Just like Fred, who had to get used to wearing long shorts, at first it might feel awkward or vulnerable. But as you ease into the change, you will start to feel lighter, more confident, and more at ease in your own skin.

Growth never happens without some friction, and leaning into that discomfort is part of the process. Don't rush to erase the awkwardness. Instead, embrace the discomfort as proof you're doing something new and worthwhile. Give yourself permission to go slow and steady—progress is still progress.

And here's the secret to making those big leaps less overwhelming: Celebrate the small wins. You don't have to wait until you've reached the summit to acknowledge your success. Every step forward is a triumph. Sent the email you were scared to write? Win. Tried a new skill and didn't nail it the first time? Still a win.

Shifting your mindset to see the victories in the journey, not just the destination, creates momentum and builds confidence. Breaking your own cornerstone rules doesn't require you to be perfect—it requires you to be persistent, curious, and kind to yourself along the way. Once you start celebrating what you *can* do, those pants won't just disappear, they'll feel like they were never there at all.

Breaking Your Cornerstone Rules

That same spirit of shaking off restrictive rules is at the heart of drag—where norms around dress and identity are turned on their head for the sake of creativity, self-expression, and fun. Drag is an art form that the Queer Community has brought into the shared culture. Anyone can put on a costume or makeup and become a superstar, even for a few hours. Outside of a Hollywood set, dressing in drag is the furthest you

Are you willing to question and break self-imposed limitations?

can get from wearing a normal outfit—it's a chance to try on a different self.

One of the most beautiful aspects of drag is that the performers aren't taking life too seriously. They are leaning into the fun of it all. Drag is a spectacle. It makes fun of society's made-up rules around gender, which place a lot of unnecessary pressure on all of us, like specific ways to act, love, and feel. Anything we can do to liberate ourselves from society's gender norms is a chance to break free from it all.

Indian transgender advocate Kalki Subramaniam describes her aunties poking fun at Queer folks for dressing hyperfeminine, with over-the-top glamour. Her response to them was, "Queer people dress for themselves, not for others." So if you ever doubt yourself as you break your cornerstone rule, remember, you are doing it for yourself, not for others.

With that in mind, here are some cornerstone rules that are meant to be broken. Look through the list, pick one, and have fun breaking it! Some will take more work than others. Some you can do today; some need a longer timeline. This is for you and no one else.

- People with my body type should/shouldn't wear ________.
- I don't dance in public.
- I never try that food or flavor.
- I'm too old/young to ______________.
- I'm not creative enough to ______________.
- I'm not smart enough to ______________.
- I'm not sexy enough to ______________.
- I'm too shy to speak up.
- I can't change careers now.
- I don't ask for help.
- I can't express my emotions.
- I don't like going to new places alone.

Many of us have grown up in a world that has kept us in line with rules around how to be. Those rules get internalized and then we impose them on ourselves and make them a cornerstone of our responses and behavior. The beauty is, you can find joy in breaking those rules.

I spent a lot of my life trying to not come across as gay. I had a cornerstone rule that I shouldn't wear clothes that made me look too feminine or flamboyant. This came from a place of internalized homophobia. Luckily, I've learned the confidence to break that rule. My circles now expect fabulousness, and I'm often the happiest when I'm serving bold sartorial choices and standout colors. Even if no one else notices, I do. I've found joy, and it's all because I broke this cornerstone rule.

IF RULES don't serve you, why follow them? Resisting change for no good reason isn't really worth it; you could be missing out on joy. Any statement you repeat about yourself that has "don't" or "can't" in it is a good indication of something that could benefit from reconsideration.

You've started to break free from the rules you've imposed on yourself—so what about the rules that shape the world around you? Many of the categories we take for granted, like gender, have been constructed to keep us in neat little boxes (LGBTQ+ Life Lesson #6). But what happens when we stop forcing ourselves to fit into binaries and start imagining a future that reflects the full spectrum of who we all are? We'll look at that in the next chapter.

YOUR RAINBOW WISDOM TOOLKIT

Instead of holding yourself back or putting limits on what you think you can accomplish or find comfort in, just try it. You might find you love it!

- Pinpoint a self-imposed rule or limit you've never questioned.

- Take one small step to defy that rule. Expect it to feel awkward, and do it anyway.

- Recognize that friction is a sign of growth, not a reason to quit.

- Don't wait for a "big win"; every tiny success fuels momentum.

- Dress for yourself! Remember, you're breaking these rules to honor your own joy—not anyone else's expectations.

MAKE THE FUTURE NONBINARY

The Queer experience reminds us that language is about embracing everyone's right to define who they are.

Please Stop Calling Me "Sir"

I spend a good chunk of my life traveling. As soon as I step onto the plane, a friendly flight attendant greets me with, "Welcome aboard, sir." As the flight progresses, the "sir" keeps coming: "Can I get you anything, sir?" or "Please put your laptop away, we're about to land, sir." It's polite and professional, and likely part of their customer service training.

But every time I hear "sir," it gives me a momentary pause. What if I wasn't a "sir"? What if my gender wasn't male, despite the way I look to them? What if I was Two-Spirit, nonbinary, genderqueer, or genderfluid? What if I were trans-feminine or a trans woman who happened to be presenting in a way they perceived as masculine? These aren't far-fetched scenarios. And yet, with just one word—"sir"—the flight attendants have labeled me without knowing me at all.

Now, I know the intentions of flight attendants aren't malicious. But good intentions don't always lead to good outcomes. For someone who's regularly misgendered, hearing that kind of assumption can feel isolating or even invalidating. It's not just a little *oops* moment; it's a reminder of how often society forces people to explain themselves or justify who they are—something no one should have to do to feel welcome, especially in a public place like transport.

I get that these terms of address like "sir" and "ma'am" are ingrained in customer service culture—they are labels or shorthand for being respectful and polite. But is it polite if it makes someone feel singled out or unwelcome? Politeness should make people feel at ease, not as though they're being publicly outed. Why do the ways we refer to each other have to be gendered anyway?

That's why I loved a moment at a comedy show I attended. The comedians, famed internet married duo Darcy & Jer, kicked things off by greeting the crowd with "Guys, gals, and nonbinary pals!" It was funny, warm, and welcoming. No assumptions, no one left out. And I couldn't help but think, why isn't this the standard everywhere?

It's not hard to be inclusive when we address people—it just takes a little effort and awareness. Instead of using "sir" or "ma'am," try some gender-neutral alternatives: "May I assist you?" "How can I help you today?" "Would you like anything from the cart?" or simply "Thank you for your patience." And rather than saying "ladies and gentlemen," which leaves some people out, consider more welcoming language like "folks," "friends," "valued guests," or "fellow community members." When I was a teacher, I called my students "humans" or "nice people" instead of "boys and girls," and it always worked out just fine. Along with not always defaulting to these polite, gendered terms of address like "sir" and "ma'am," I suggest we all start to use the pronouns "they" and "them" more too.

Is "They" Awkward?

The pronouns "he" and "she" don't work for everyone anymore, so there's been a growing push to use "they" and "them" as pronouns more universally. Unfortunately, there is pushback against that—including from people who claim it's grammatically incorrect. But most of the time, this isn't an argument about grammar. It's often a cover for something darker—a reluctance to embrace gender diversity or to be inclusive.

My usual response to the "grammar" argument is, who cares? Language is always evolving. The singular "they" has been in use since the fourteenth century—it was borrowed from Old Norse—and has been used in English for centuries. It's not some newfangled invention. Maybe it's time to start thinking about how we want to shape the future of language instead of paralyzing it.

The truth is, you've already used "they" as a singular pronoun your whole life, maybe without realizing it. When you see someone walking down the street from far away and you can't make out their face or features, you naturally say, "That's them over there!" Or "They're wearing a stunning jacket."

The reason this feels natural is that gender neutrality is already baked into the English language. If someone tries to convince you otherwise with "grammar rules," remember that those are rules they've *chosen* to follow. In fact, all the contemporary style guides have already embraced inclusive language. For example, *The Chicago Manual of Style*—often considered the copyediting "bible"—explicitly supports the use of the singular "they" and encourages writers to be thoughtful and inclusive in their language choices. And if Shakespeare and Chaucer could use "they" in *The Canterbury Tales* and *The Comedy of Errors*, so can you. Using "they" is not just inclusive—it's downright literary.

What's really silly is how much time people spend debating whether other folks should call themselves "she" or "he" rather than "they." Let's be honest, this debate isn't about pronouns. It's about holding on to the gender binary because that's how people have learned to organize the world in their head. Restricting pronouns is about restricting people. It's about control.

Shape the future of language instead of paralyzing it.

That doesn't mean it's wrong to feel happy and comfortable with the "he" or "she" you were assigned at birth. That's great if it works for you. But it doesn't work for everyone. And none of us have the right to control how other people define themselves. And that includes their pronouns.

So how do you start making your language more open and inclusive? One easy way is to use "they" and "them" more freely—not just for individuals, but within groups too. For example, instead of saying, "Each guest should pick up his or her drink," try, "Each guest should pick up their drink." It's simple and elegant, and it removes unnecessary barriers from your language.

When you're talking about someone you don't know personally—like the barista making your coffee or the driver who let you merge—try resisting the instinct to assign them "she" or "he." Instead, use "they." You might say, "Their latte art is amazing" or "They just made my day by letting me cut in." Not only does this make your language more thoughtful, it also trains your brain to approach people with curiosity instead of assumption.

At first, this might feel awkward. Like any habit, it takes practice. But over time, the meaningful shift becomes second nature. This small change in how we speak can make the world feel more inclusive and start breaking down rigid ideas about gender that just don't serve us. And it's not just about pronouns—it's about making space for everyone to show up as themselves. And that's a world worth working toward.

Beyond Binary

One of the world's most notable Queer and nonbinary advocates, Alok Vaid-Menon, has talked a lot about the pressure we all face to stay locked into being *either* male or female. Alok is a well-known artist and advocate who challenges and deconstructs binary gender norms. Alok uses they/them pronouns and is celebrated for their contributions to transgender, nonbinary, gender fluidity, and body positivity awareness.

Part of Alok's story has been the backlash they faced for failing to fulfill the gender role traps set up by those around them. In Alok's book *Beyond the Gender Binary*, they discuss never satisfying gender expectations imposed on them by others. Alok, assigned male at birth, was often criticized and called "a girl" for being too expressive and not presenting in traditional masculine ways. Then, when they came out as Queer and nonbinary, finally embracing the femininity that many had already been labeling them with, they were ridiculed for not being feminine enough and called a "boy." Talk about a lose-lose situation. They couldn't win. As Alok says, "The gender binary is set up for us to fail. For us all to fail."

Alok is not alone in highlighting these restrictive, lose-lose gender expectations. Decades earlier, American Queer Black civil rights advocate and writer James Baldwin also recognized how dividing the world solely into "man" and "woman" forces everyone into confining labels:

> The American ideal, then, of sexuality appears to be rooted in the American ideal of masculinity. This ideal has created cowboys and Indians, good guys and bad guys, punks and studs, tough guys and softies, butch and faggot, black and white. It is an ideal so paralytically infantile that it is virtually forbidden—as an unpatriotic act—that the American boy evolve into the complexity of manhood . . . but once you have discerned the meaning of a label, it may seem to define you for others, but it does not have the power to define you to yourself.

What Baldwin is saying is that we are programmed to think of ourselves in a binary way from a young age: us versus them, success versus failure. This approach limits everyone to the title they are given. The result is that this binary thinking creates walls that keep everyone from the complexity and variety life has to offer.

So what do we do about these binary limitations? Well, we break free from them, together.

Breaking free from the male–female binary isn't just a struggle for trans and nonbinary people, though; the fight for gender freedom involves everyone—straight, cisgender, trans, Two-Spirit, Queer, agender, and nonbinary people alike. It's about freeing us all from outdated ideas about gender that were imposed on us even before we were born.

Gender Reveal Parties Are Silly

Let's face it: Gender reveal parties need an update. And, no, it's not just because some people think exploding a balloon filled with blue or pink glitter is peak entertainment. The whole concept is misleading from the start. It's not a "gender reveal" party—it's actually an "anatomy reveal" party. What you're actually announcing is a baby's biological sex based on an ultrasound technician's snapshot of their anatomy, not who the baby is or will be. Gender, unlike anatomical sex, is about identity—it's how someone feels and expresses themselves in the world. And trust me, a fetus doesn't send out vibes about their future gender identity while in the womb.

Why are we still stuck in this 1950s color-coding of pink for girls and blue for boys, anyway? A baby doesn't care what color their onesie is; they just want food and sleep. This color-coding drives the outdated notion that girls and boys are supposed to like different things from birth. Limiting a kid's options before they even get to choose is like locking them into a personality box they never signed up for. It's setting up a world where we think gender identity is based on silly things like color and toy preferences in childhood, and then things like jobs or who we are attracted to later on in life.

Babies are tiny humans who will grow into complex individuals with their own thoughts, feelings, and, yes, gender identities. Some kids might grow up and align perfectly with the blue or pink box—others will not. If they don't, this can lead to feelings of confusion, rejection, or being forced into an identity that doesn't feel right. This stifles their growth and creates barriers to exploring who they are.

In the end, gender reveal parties reinforce the idea that there are only two ways to be: boy or girl. Anyone who doesn't fit neatly into those boxes is automatically "othered." It reinforces harmful gender norms and excludes people who don't relate to the cisnormative binary. Why not give kids the freedom to decide who they are when they're ready?

Whatever you decide to call your party, I suggest you avoid referring to it as a "gender reveal party," because it really isn't: A person's gender belongs to them, not their parents or parents' friends. I'm not saying don't have a party to celebrate the good news, but call it an "anatomy reveal" party instead. Although you can see how that could get weird: "My baby has a penis!" or "My baby has a vagina!" So how about just announcing it's a healthy human? "Congratulations, it's a human" has a timely and compassionate ring to it. And then raise your children in a way that makes it perfectly clear to them, and the world around you, that they can define their gender however they want.

If Shakespeare
and Chaucer could
use "they/them,"
so can you.

Gender Fluidity Pre-Colonization

Our primary caregivers often have a lot to do with how gender gets defined for us. Fortunately, many Indigenous ancestors give us guidance on how to look at the binary of gender in more open-minded ways.

The gender binary—the idea that only two genders exist—was not always a universal concept. Colonizers, particularly Christian Europeans, forced these strict definitions onto Indigenous, Black, and other racialized people. Prior to colonization, many cultures worldwide embraced more fluid understandings of gender and sexuality.

In North America, many First Nations honored individuals who embodied both masculine and feminine qualities. Today, some of those individuals use the pan-Indigenous term "Two-Spirit" to refer to themselves. Historically, numerous First Nations revered Two-Spirit people as spiritual leaders, healers, and community guides, holding significant roles within their nations—a tradition that continues to this day.

In South Asia, the hijra community has thrived for thousands of years, recognized as a third gender deeply interwoven with Hindu mythology and cultural practices.

In precolonial Africa, the Igbo people of Nigeria acknowledged gender fluidity through figures such as "female husbands"—women who took on male social roles and even married other women.

Polynesian cultures also celebrated gender diversity. In Hawaii and Tahiti, māhū—individuals embodying both masculine and feminine traits—often served as healers and keepers of cultural knowledge. Meanwhile, in Samoa, fa'afafine have long been recognized as a third gender.

In parts of South America, including some Andean societies, Indigenous groups connected gender diversity to spiritual and ceremonial roles. In Chile, machis are Mapuche shamans and spiritual leaders who embody multiple genders to fulfill ritual purposes in their communities.

In Southeast Asia, the Bugis people of Indonesia recognize five distinct genders: masculine men, feminine women, calalai (masculine females), calabai (feminine males), and bissu, who represent a harmonious blend of all genders.

Even in the Middle East, pre-Islamic Arabia acknowledged gender-nonconformity through the mukhannathūn, who performed in royal courts. Although later eras imposed more rigid social norms, Queer identities still surface in medieval Islamic and Middle Eastern literature, history, and culture.

These are just some of the many examples that exist around the world. In some societies, the tradition of celebrating gender diversity remains. In others, these teachings are being reclaimed as part of decolonization and the assertion of sovereignty. For example, the Two-Spirit movement in North America continues to grow in recognition and validation. In India, laws are finally being rewritten and decolonized to reflect the gender-diversity inclusion that predated British invasion.

Sadly, in regions where colonial laws displaced gender-queer communities, homophobia and transphobia now run rampant. It is ironic that many former colonizing countries—such as the United Kingdom, France, the Netherlands, Spain, Portugal, and Belgium—are now among the world's safest places for Queer people, while the homophobic and transphobic laws they once imposed still harm the nations they colonized. Queerphobia is, in many ways, a brutal legacy of colonialism.

Some people mistakenly claim that Queerness is a Western concept, yet the evidence tells a different story. In truth, it was homophobia, transphobia, and queerphobia that the Global West exported to much of the world.

How to Break Free

You'd think that with the rise of feminism and justice movements worldwide, more people would be eager to break down old gender norms. The trouble is that most people don't love change. It's comforting to stick with what feels familiar, the world as they've always known it. For these people, their identity is deeply tied to being a "man" or a "woman," and when those categories are questioned, it can feel unsettling, even threatening.

That's why these conversations need to be framed in ways that aren't about taking anything away from anyone. Instead, let's talk about creating more space—space for people to define themselves, to choose the label (or no label) that feels right for them. It's not about erasing gender; it's about giving everyone the freedom to decide what their gender means for *themselves*.

If someone feels happy and fulfilled being a man or a woman in the traditional sense, that's great. We should celebrate that. And we should also celebrate those who step outside those lines, who define their own gender on their own terms. Everyone deserves that same sense of freedom.

Here's how I see it: My gender is mine—not yours, not society's, not anyone else's. Affirming someone's gender is about respect. It's about honoring their choice to live authentically, instead of forcing them to conform to a narrow set of rules that don't fit. In that way, gender-nonconforming, genderqueer, transgender, and nonbinary people are a kind of trailblazer. By showing us the way, they help all of us feel freer—freer to be exactly who we are.

DIVIDING THE WORLD UP exclusively into the binaries of "she" and "he" doesn't work. Instead, let's create a future that includes everyone. By being willing to improve the way we describe each other, we might feel more compelled to respect each other, and when we respect each other, we're more likely to stand up for each other. We'll talk about the steps we can take to maximize our allyship in LGBTQ+ Life Lesson #15.

YOUR RAINBOW WISDOM TOOLKIT

Here are some ways to step outside gender binaries that restrict everyone:

- Skip "sir" or "ma'am" and choose non-gendered greetings and language—no one should be boxed in by assumptions.

- Remember that the gender-neutral pronoun "they" is centuries old and is already used in everyday speech; it welcomes all identities.

- Gender is personal—let people choose their own labels (or none at all).

- Queerphobia was exported globally; many cultures originally honored diverse genders.

- Celebrate everyone's freedom to exist beyond "he" and "she," as we work toward a truly inclusive future.

LGBTQ+ LIFE LESSON #15

STAND TOGETHER

The Queer Community
teaches everyone
that solidarity in the
face of confrontation is
a profound act of love.

Lesbians to the Rescue

In the early 1980s, a mysterious and deadly disease began to spread through various communities, leaving heartache and loss in its wake. It had no name at first—just fearful whispers of an unknown threat. Within the gay community, anxiety grew quickly. Friends became ill, yet no one understood why. Fear led to isolation as stigma took hold in society. For gay men, it felt as if the world was turning its back exactly when they most needed compassion. One haunting truth became clear: They were alone in their fight.

The US government's initial response ranged from indifference to open hostility. President Ronald Reagan did not publicly discuss AIDS until 1987, six years after the crisis began and after over twenty thousand Americans had died. Even then, his remarks suggested moral judgment rather than real commitment to medical intervention. In a speech to the American Foundation for AIDS Research, he said, "When it comes to preventing AIDS, don't medicine and morality teach the same lessons?" This framing painted AIDS as a result of personal behavior, reinforcing stigma rather than prompting urgent government action. In Canada, the official reaction was similarly lethargic. Public health agencies and politicians hesitated, delaying crucial research and funding even as thousands died.

Dubbed the "gay plague" by the media, AIDS became a label that stoked public fears and justified inaction. Conservative commentator Pat Buchanan declared, "The poor homosexuals—they have declared war upon nature, and now nature is exacting an awful retribution." Such viewpoints rippled through mainstream discourse. Gay men, already battling a lethal virus, had to navigate widespread hostility and rejection. Even within health care institutions, many faced denial of care. There are accounts of nurses skipping the rooms of AIDS patients entirely, leaving meals on the floor, or not changing the sheets. Families, sometimes motivated by shame or fear, abandoned their ailing sons too. For too many, dying alone or in unsanitary conditions was the final cruelty.

Into this void of compassion, lesbians stepped forward as heroes. Although gay men and lesbians often moved in distinct social circles, the AIDS crisis sparked a new spirit of unity. Lesbians organized blood drives, food deliveries, sat at hospital bedsides, cared for orphaned pets, and fought for better health care for AIDS patients. They refused to stand by while their brothers suffered—they were needed, and they showed up. These acts of support went far beyond logistics; many gay men described the care from lesbians as their sole comfort in those darkest days.

Lesbians did more than show up at hospital bedsides. They also served as advocates and organizers, building networks to provide meals, transportation, and a compassionate presence during men's final days. The Lesbian Herstory Archives in Brooklyn holds numerous letters from gay men expressing gratitude for the simple gifts of care—like being fed or bathed when they no longer had the strength to do it themselves.

Stories of lesbians standing in for estranged families at funerals, comforting grieving partners, or accompanying men to doctors' offices became legendary. They provided essential, tender support: holding the hands of dying men, writing obituaries, and battling for access to medication. Over time, these stories became icons of an unbreakable bond. The AIDS crisis also sparked a cultural shift in the LGBTQ+ community itself. Even amid collective grief, there was a flourishing sense of pride and solidarity. The term "Queer" was reclaimed as a badge of resistance, uniting a fractured community beneath one empowering banner.

From tragedy grew a deeper sense of responsibility within the Queer Community. Yes, a generation was devastated, but the crisis also birthed a movement rooted in resilience, love, and steadfast solidarity. It's a story of how Queer people, largely abandoned by mainstream society, discovered their greatest strength in each other and redefined what it means to be allies.

We Won't Be Divided

"Divide and conquer"—fragmenting the opposition into smaller, more easily controlled segments—is a well-worn strategy of those who feel threatened. It's no surprise that those who seek to undo Queer liberation often try to fracture the unity of the Queer Community itself.

In recent years, conservative political entities have zeroed in on genderqueer, gender-diverse, and transgender individuals. They aim to divide the rainbow in half, isolating sexuality from gender diversity. This tactic is evident in transphobic content that selectively omits the "T," proclaiming support for LGB rights but ignoring or denying transgender people's needs.

I've even encountered angry gay men who challenge my support for gender-diverse people, warning that this alliance risks eroding the rights we've fought so hard to secure for ourselves as gay men. This is exactly what oppressors want: to make us so fearful that we sacrifice someone else's rights to preserve our own sense of safety. Fortunately, I see the vast majority of Queer people rejecting this temptation. Instead, they stand confidently with transgender, nonbinary, Two-Spirit, and genderqueer people.

There are many reasons for this solidarity. One of the most central is the realization that it's impossible to separate sexuality from gender within many Queer experiences. Some individuals identify primarily with one aspect—perhaps just sexuality or just gender—but for a large part of the community, the journey of coming out and coming to terms with yourself reveals that the constructs of gender and sexuality are indeed just that: constructs.

Though I'm not transgender, I know that the patriarchal binary foisted upon us never quite fit me. I feel like a man, but my version of "man" is a much Queerer vision than many gender-deniers could accept. In standing with transgender, nonbinary, and genderqueer people, I also stand up for my own, more expansive sense of gender identity. Their bravery in claiming their authenticity paves the way for me to do the same.

Plenty of Queer individuals embrace the term "Queer" because it's intentionally broad—it signals a wide range of sexual and gender diversity, without forcing constant explanation. Why should we have to clarify all the details of our personal, intimate identity? "Queer" asserts difference from the norm without revealing every nuanced part of who we are.

My solidarity is driven in some part by a historical perspective. When I once posted about the Stonewall Riots, a troll commented, "Trans people weren't even at Stonewall— why do you care about them?" Simply put, the troll was both ignorant and wrong. Transgender people, although that term wasn't widely used at the time, were undeniably present. A

**To see ourselves in
others is not only
an act of compassion
but a survival strategy.**

careful reading of the archives confirms that the Queer Liberation movement has always been about freeing humanity from oppressive rules regarding who we can love (sexuality) and how we can live and express ourselves (gender). The story of Marsha P. Johnson, mentioned in the chapter on Queer Joy (LGBTQ+ Life Lesson #8), is just one example of a genderqueer individual occupying an honored role in the history of Queerness.

Perhaps the simplest reason for solidarity is that most Queer people know what it feels like to be marginalized and misunderstood. We know what it's like to realize the world isn't built for us. When Queer folks and allies stand side by side, it reflects our commitment to uphold inclusion and fight for the kind of change that benefits us all.

But what about Queer people who don't stand with others in their community—such as a gay person who rejects the notion of Queerness altogether, denies gender diversity, or focuses solely on sexuality diversity? That does happen. Yet I've never met a trans person who denies the existence of gay people. This kind of refusal is typically linked to privilege.

Some Queer people turn against their own and become willing mouthpieces for discrimination. Discriminators are eager to parade a gay person who opposes gay rights or a trans person who speaks against transgender rights—similar to when a person of color claims racism is a myth. While these individuals exist, they do not represent the majority. When an overwhelming number of people in a marginalized group share lived experiences of oppression, it's vital we listen instead of looking for excuses to deny.

Certainly, there are small factions of gay people who rally against gay rights, or gays who oppose transgender rights, or even trans people who fight the extension of rights to other trans individuals. I won't spotlight them here because I don't wish to amplify their perspectives. However, I have observed a common thread among Queer individuals who undermine the inclusion of others: They're often grappling with significant trauma or have been ostracized by the community themselves. When someone is treated badly and can't find community support, they may lash out by aligning with those who foster discrimination. It's a heartbreaking reality.

The saddest part comes when queerphobic discriminators, itching to have someone from the Queer Community justify their actions, welcome an "injured bird" with open arms, providing what looks like acceptance but is actually exploitation. The Queer person who was rejected finally feels seen, but their new "allies" see them only as a tool to further discrimination. I share this not to demonize those who are hurting but to highlight how the tactic of using defectors is classic divide-and-conquer strategy. As Audre Lorde, the self-described "black, lesbian, mother, warrior, poet," wrote: "If I didn't define myself for myself, I would be crunched into other people's fantasies for me and eaten alive."

I raise these sad scenarios because anti-Queer groups often use such stories to weaken Queer liberation. The internet gives everyone a microphone—so you can always find a "gay person" who doesn't like other gays or a "transphobic trans person"—but that doesn't mean their views negate the experiences of countless Queer people who simply want acceptance, love, and support.

Solidarity Must Prevail

It's easy to let our guard down when it comes to inclusion. Life can be tough, and when we're under pressure, it's natural to focus on our own survival rather than fighting for broader equity. This is not just an individual failing; it's a symptom of living in a society that profits from keeping people divided. We're trained to zero in on surface differences rather than seek out commonalities.

Gunther von Hagens, a German anatomist, dramatically demonstrated our shared humanity through the *Body Worlds* exhibits, using plastination to preserve the bodies of deceased people. Visitors could see muscles, organs, and tissues in vivid detail. While startling—even shocking—this display offered a powerful reminder that beneath the external differences we fixate on, we are almost indistinguishable. We can't see someone's religion, sexuality, gender, or race by simply peering at their muscles and bones. Under the skin, our similarities are striking.

Many institutions benefit from hiding this shared humanity. Religions have often been used to cast certain groups as "other," sowing division instead of promoting unity. Politicians capitalize on these divisions to stay in power, encouraging us to fear or distrust each other rather than challenge the systems that harm us all.

History offers a stark reminder of the dangers of division. In times of genocide, war, and famine, the victims almost always share the same heartbreaking insight: As the grip of starvation tightens or the threat of death looms, the distinctions that once seemed so important disappear. Indeed, we are all human. Recognizing this truth is essential to understanding how those in power manipulate us. Division isn't just a side effect of inequality; it's a tool used to perpetuate it. It's why every move to weaken justice and equity must be met with vigilance—not just against the systems that seek to divide, but against our own internalized biases.

Pastor Martin Niemöller illustrated this starkly in his famous post-Holocaust reflection:

First they came for the socialists, and I did not speak out—because I was not a socialist. Then they came for the trade unionists, and I did not speak out—because I was not a trade unionist. Then they came for the Jews, and I did not speak out—because I was not a Jew. Then they came for me—and there was no one left to speak for me.

These lines are more than a warning; they're a call to action. To see ourselves in others is not just an act of compassion, but a survival strategy. If we wait until the harm reaches our doorstep, it's already too late. Solidarity isn't optional; it's essential. It's time we stop seeing "them" and start seeing "us."

Stronger (and More Fun) Together

The beauty of allyship shows itself in collective action. Everyone feels vulnerable when alone. Think of fish traveling in schools, birds in flocks, or sheep in herds—they survive by moving together. There is an inherent safety in numbers.

Nation-states have always recognized this principle. Alliances such as the European Union, African Union, NATO, or the Soviet Bloc highlight the understanding that without mutual support, we're exposed to aggression, financial instability, and threats no single country can address by itself. Whether for defense, trade, or diplomacy, these agreements prove that cooperation isn't just a strategy—it's essential for survival in an interconnected world. It's important to harness this power of unity in our personal lives as well, not only during crises but in good times too.

Courage isn't just about being first. Have you ever noticed the power of allyship on the dance floor? Imagine someone stepping onto a completely empty dance floor. Their boldness

It's time we stop
seeing "them" and
start seeing "us."

is evident—they stand alone, unafraid to be seen. But without someone else joining them, their act remains an isolated display, more a curiosity than a celebration.

When someone else steps onto the floor, something changes. That second person becomes a bridge, transforming the moment from a solitary act into a shared invitation. This person effectively says, "This is worth joining." Their participation gives onlookers permission to do the same, shifting the focus from a lone dancer to a gathering movement.

We often admire the first as the one with courage, and that's fair. But their role is to start the story, to create the possibility. It's the second person—the ally—who makes that possibility real. The person who joins in gives others permission to follow, turning an isolated dancer into collective action. Without them, the first remains alone, their bravery unnoticed, their idea unrealized. Movements thrive on allies who see the spark, jump up to join, and fan it into a flame.

So be bold and become that second person—the ally—and watch how quickly a movement can ignite.

How to Show Up as an Ally

Standing beside someone who faces discrimination can be intimidating. Perhaps you worry the hostility might be turned on you, or you simply dislike conflict. Both concerns are understandable. That's why I teach the concept of the Allyship Ladder. It offers different levels of risk and corresponding rewards for both you and the person you're supporting. The higher the rung, the greater the potential impact, but also the greater the vulnerability. It's the classic risk–reward balance.

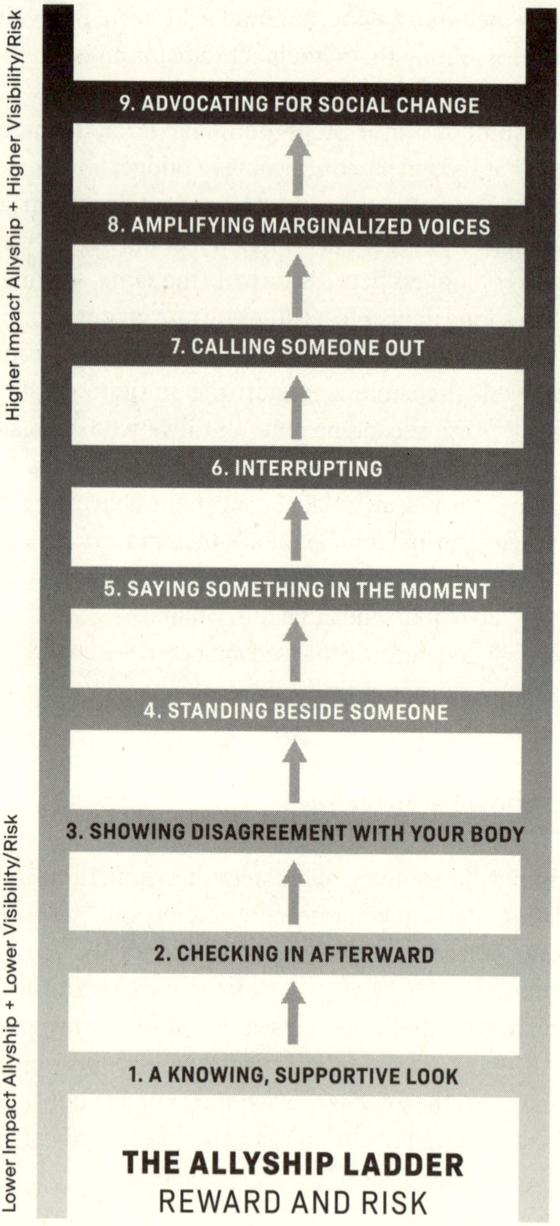

Higher Impact Allyship + Higher Visibility/Risk
Lower Impact Allyship + Lower Visibility/Risk
9. ADVOCATING FOR SOCIAL CHANGE
8. AMPLIFYING MARGINALIZED VOICES
7. CALLING SOMEONE OUT
6. INTERRUPTING
5. SAYING SOMETHING IN THE MOMENT
4. STANDING BESIDE SOMEONE
3. SHOWING DISAGREEMENT WITH YOUR BODY
2. CHECKING IN AFTERWARD
1. A KNOWING, SUPPORTIVE LOOK
THE ALLYSHIP LADDER
REWARD AND RISK

The Allyship Ladder: Reward and Risk

The Allyship Ladder progresses from low-risk, low-visibility gestures to high-risk, high-visibility advocacy. Each rung offers a way to reflect on how you can best show up, given the circumstances.

A Knowing, Supportive Look: Sometimes, the smallest act can mean the world. A simple, understanding glance says, "I see you, and I'm here," without using any words.

Reward: Offers immediate reassurance to someone who feels vulnerable, building trust and emotional support.

Checking In Afterward: Reaching out after a hurtful incident is a low-risk way to say you care. Even if you couldn't intervene at the time, sending a message or making a call lets the other person know they aren't alone.

Reward: Strengthens your relationship and opens the door to plan for better responses in the future.

Showing Disagreement with Your Body: Nonverbal gestures—crossed arms, a shake of the head, or walking away—can convey disapproval and shift the energy of the situation.

Reward: Signals clear boundaries to the perpetrator and bystanders, helping defuse tension.

Standing Beside Someone So They Feel Less Alone: Physically placing yourself next to someone who's being targeted speaks volumes. Words may fail you, but being visibly present can significantly disrupt discrimination.

Reward: Offers emotional support to the person targeted and serves as an example of real solidarity in action.

Saying Something in the Moment: Speaking up—like saying, "That's not okay"—takes more courage because it places you in the spotlight.

Reward: Demonstrates your allyship publicly, empowering the targeted individual and often encouraging bystanders to join you.

Interrupting: Stepping in to halt discriminatory behavior on the spot requires decisiveness. This might mean redirecting the discussion or asking for a pause.

Reward: Can quickly defuse the situation, potentially preventing further harm.

Calling Someone Out: Confronting the offender's behavior in a public or group setting shows a strong commitment to accountability. It's high-profile and may spark intense reactions.

Reward: Exposes unacceptable conduct and sets a precedent that such behavior won't be tolerated, paving the way for education.

Amplifying Marginalized Voices: Use your platform—social media, community groups, or other spaces—to uplift the perspectives of people directly affected by discrimination. Rather than speaking for them, help their voices reach a wider audience.

Reward: Validates their experiences and ensures that their needs and solutions become the priority.

Advocating for Social Change: Engaging in activism (organizing events, speaking at rallies, influencing policies) is a long-term commitment to systemic allyship. It takes sustained effort. Part of this work involves educating yourself and collaborating with those most affected so the solutions genuinely address their needs.

Reward: Contributes to lasting social change, building more inclusive systems and communities for future generations.

The Allyship Ladder is a tool to spark both reflection and action. While each rung builds on the last, you can step onto it at any level. No matter where you begin, your efforts move us closer to a society where everyone belongs. Of course, always consider your immediate safety and that of others, especially in dangerous situations. If necessary, involve additional allies or contact authorities to minimize harm.

ALLYSHIP IS A unifying force that protects and enriches us all. By standing strong against attempts to divide us, we come to recognize our shared humanity. And when you remind others they're not alone, you discover you aren't alone either. Unity builds resilience, fostering the momentum needed for meaningful, lasting change.

Now that we've explored what it means to stand (and dance) together, let's see how to reshape our world through collective action, in LGBTQ+ Life Lesson #16.

YOUR RAINBOW WISDOM TOOLKIT

When pondering your own allyship, remember these things:

- Opponents will try to pit marginalized groups against each other. Refuse to let them fracture solidarity.

- Draw strength from shared humanity; showing up for each other builds resilience and prevents isolation.

- Use the Allyship Ladder: Pick the level of allyship you can offer, from a simple supportive glance to public advocacy, and keep climbing.

- Refuse to sacrifice anyone's rights. Don't let fear make you trade someone else's safety for your own sense of security.

- Remember, whether on a dance floor or in social movements, the real momentum comes when we stand with others.

INCLUSION MAKES ALL LIVES BETTER

When the world is designed with inclusion in mind, we make life better for everyone.

A Northern Lesson in Inclusion

Nestled in the remote reaches of northern Alberta, brushing the Northwest Territories, lies the town of Fort Chipewyan, set within the sprawling wilderness of Wood Buffalo National Park—the largest national park in Canada. This expanse of untamed beauty, where the land and waters stretch endlessly beneath a sky of shimmering northern lights, is accessible for most of the year only by plane or boat. The journey becomes a thrilling adventure during the winter months when the rivers freeze to form a sturdy ice road. Fort Chipewyan is a mosaic of cultures, predominantly the Mikisew Cree First Nation, Athabasca Chipewyan First Nation, and Métis Nation, but it is also home to individuals from diverse backgrounds.

This region carries a complicated history marked by horrific acts of genocide against Indigenous peoples. Once bustling with thriving land-based cultures, it has experienced deep disruption and trauma due to colonization. Numerous Christian residential and day schools aimed to erase Indigenous identities and force assimilation. First Nations that once moved seasonally, following the land's natural rhythms for hunting, fishing, and gathering, were forced to stay in one place, confined to government-imposed reserves around Fort Chipewyan. Many families also relocated to be closer to their children, who were imprisoned in residential schools. This upheaval severed traditional ways of life and disrupted many people's deep connection to the land.

However, this is not the only narrative of the region. During my visit, I encountered a tight-knit, collaborative, and welcoming community that exemplifies resilience and strength in the face of oppression. The community's isolation unites people and fosters a sense of pride in a home nestled in the wilderness that few outsiders ever visit.

Some would expect that, due to its isolation and colonial history, this remote corner of the world wouldn't show any signs of 2SLGBTQ+ pride and inclusion; yet this was one of the first places in mostly conservative Alberta to paint a rainbow crosswalk in their town. They wanted to signal inclusion, support, and welcome for Two-Spirit, Indigiqueer, and Queer Community members.

The heartwarming part of the story is that no locals objected to it. As I got to know the town's Elders and community leaders, I discovered that no one had a problem with the rainbow crosswalk when it was first painted. They understood that pride symbols are meant to signal safe space and respect—not recruitment, as those opposed might try to spin it. They recognized that the rainbow crosswalk was there to ensure everyone felt comfortable in their hometown.

The crosswalk was never an issue until a group of out-of-towners arrived and began criticizing Queer inclusion. Their objections and mockery stirred up complaints, and what had once been a harmonious decision became a point of conflict. A town that had embraced inclusion suddenly found itself divided by outside negativity. Fortunately, the community stood by the crosswalk, but the seeds of discord had been sown by those who came from elsewhere.

It was refreshing to learn that communities can be designed to be inclusive even when we don't always expect them to be.

However, that work can just as easily be undone through the enticing power of exclusion. We can find ways to resist that temptation.

Universal Design

Universal design seeks to create inclusive spaces that promote equality and ease of use, ensuring that everyone can participate fully in society. The great thing is that universal design makes life better for everyone, not just for those who need it to get by.

Universal design happens when architects make a building work for everyone who uses it, no matter what abilities they have or do not have. It's a given nowadays that we'll have elevators that work for people who have vision differences, and ramps that accommodate those who use wheelchairs. It's also the reason we have tactile indicators on sidewalks, and intuitive, user-friendly interfaces in technology.

All sorts of people choose to use ramps to enter spaces, not just those in wheelchairs. Lots of people love technology that is more intuitive, not just those with sensory issues. How many of us benefit from voice navigation apps that offer hands-free, turn-by-turn directions, making road trips easier and safer for all—not only those with visual impairments? Accessible playgrounds mean that kids with disabilities can play, but so can everyone else in new and varied ways. Lever handles on doors were first designed for people who had trouble gripping round handles, but now we all use them gratefully when our hands are full or too dirty.

The idea is that when we design well, we are not just accommodating a few; we are enhancing the experience for all. This philosophy of inclusivity is not only about meeting

Design a future
that leaves
no one behind.

needs—it's about designing for a future that leaves no one behind. We can design our communities with universal design as well. It's a worthy challenge to think of our communities in ways that ensure everyone can participate, instead of only the privileged.

In the same way, Queer folks have discovered new methods of creating Queer spaces that are more inclusive, making room for everyone to breathe more deeply. This doesn't mean we're letting go of one set of rules just to bind ourselves to another; it means creating spaces that can include everyone.

Universal Design as Inclusion for Queer People

All around the world, there are countless examples of Queer people being excluded from public life and spaces. Those who seek to suppress Queerness often do so by restricting access to spaces that all people rely on and deserve access to, turning them into inhospitable environments for Queer people—places like washrooms, changerooms, sports teams, and schools. Even in some supposedly inclusive communities, transgender people are forced to use the washroom corresponding to their assigned birth gender rather than the gender in which they live their lives, exposing them to potential violence or exclusion.

Opposition to trans inclusion rarely announces itself openly; instead, it cloaks itself in "concern," in questions of "safety" and "fairness." But scratch the surface and a familiar pattern emerges: Trans people are cast as threats. Generally, those who oppose trans inclusion weave a web of fear around trans people, portraying them as a threat to the safety, comfort, or innocence of others—particularly women and children. This narrative is not based on evidence but on long-standing stereotypes and fabricated moral panic. Trans people are falsely cast as predators or infiltrators in spaces like washrooms and changerooms, yet there is no statistical evidence to support these claims.

What many people don't realize is that portraying Queer people as a risk to safety is a well-established strategy of exclusion. These misinformation campaigns targeting trans people today are similar to the arguments once used to exclude gay people. Just like back then, the withholding of Queer rights is justified through harmful lies about protecting the safety of the general public. The irony is that it is Queer people who are most at risk for violence and harm, yet few governments intervene to protect them. Instead, they respond to fear-farmed hysteria to justify excluding Queer folks from rights and public life.

So how do we get out of this mess?

A great way forward is to look at the principles of universal design. Instead of focusing on ways to exclude people, we need to figure out how we can include everyone. Rather than promoting the idea that Queer people are a danger in public spaces like washrooms, the universal design principle would ask, "What can we do to make washrooms safer and more inclusive for everyone?"

Welcoming Everyone

It's not just sports organizations like Hockey Canada (which I talked about in LGBTQ+ Life Lesson #4) that are rethinking traditional spaces. Many new public spaces, including restaurants, airports, shopping malls, and schools, are moving away from the standard "men's rooms" and "women's rooms" model. This shift addresses a deeper issue: Gender-diverse people often face a dilemma between being true to their gender—how they feel in their heart and present themselves to the world—or adhering to the sex assigned on their first birth certificate. After all, why should people be segregated based on their genitalia when no one sees each other's private parts in a public washroom?

Many modern restrooms are designed to be gender-free, featuring single, floor-to-ceiling stalls that offer privacy and safety for everyone, regardless of gender. In these universal designs, central common sink and mirror areas are available to everyone as soon as they exit their own private stall. This design increases overall safety by eliminating isolated spaces where people could be trapped or vulnerable. This setup not only ensures privacy but also fosters a sense of security.

Research published by Cambridge University Press backs this up. They found that well-designed, open-concept, single-stall washrooms can increase safety and privacy. But it doesn't stop there! They also discovered that these gender-free washrooms can reduce overall waiting time too! And everyone can get behind shorter bathroom lines!

This is a great example of how redesigning spaces to include some who may be left out actually makes them better for others.

It's at this point where some trans-exclusionary folks usually say that allowing transgender women into washrooms or other gender-segregated spaces exposes other women to risk. But insisting that someone assigned male at birth is more likely to perpetrate violence against women is a cop-out. No sign on a bathroom stall is going to prevent anyone from committing violence, and if society is truly concerned about men being violent against women, we should take collective approaches to reduce the precursors to violence instead of unfairly scapegoating trans women as perpetrators of violence in their own washrooms.

Designating a bathroom as "women's only" doesn't prevent threats at all, but it can create a false sense of security. The vast majority of assaults that occur in women's change-rooms have nothing to do with transgender women.

In fact, there's no evidence that including trans people in the washroom that matches their affirmed gender affects safety. The Williams Institute at UCLA School of Law has conducted research indicating that gender identity–inclusive non-discrimination laws do not compromise safety or privacy in public facilities. They analyzed criminal incident reports and concluded there was no increase in privacy or safety violations in public restrooms, locker rooms, or changing rooms following the enactment of inclusion when transgender people are welcomed. Their evidence suggests that concerns that transgender individuals—particularly transgender women in women's restrooms—pose a threat are not empirically supported and are actually fake news.

Rather than unfairly stigmatizing transgender women as a potential risk, we should focus on making all bathrooms and changerooms safe for everyone— and gender-free washrooms are a way to do that.

Research released by the University of British Columbia School of Nursing backs the same exciting finding that inclusion makes life better for everyone. They discovered that making schools safer for Queer kids actually reduces bullying and violence for *all* kids, again making school safer for everyone.

Universal design offers more options to more people. It's the right thing to do.

DISCRIMINATION IS often justified as respect for old traditions or as protection from a threat, but the proof usually isn't there to support that perspective. Instead, we can all look for ways to design a world that is inclusive for everyone, not just the few. Since we've now taken a look at the future of Queer inclusion, let's take a moment to look at the past as well. Some important clues for a better life are waiting for us there, in LGBTQ+ Life Lesson #17.

YOUR RAINBOW WISDOM TOOLKIT

Here are some ways to increase inclusion in your own life:

- Embrace universal design (like gender-free washrooms) so all people can participate and feel safe.

- Don't buy into fear-based myths about "protecting" spaces; evidence shows inclusion doesn't compromise safety.

- Recognize that discrimination is often disguised as preserving tradition or promoting safety. Demand real proof instead of accepting fearmongering.

- Whenever possible, opt for policies and designs that bring more people in rather than shutting anyone out.

TELL MORE QUEER STORIES

Let's change the way
we talk about humanity's
past so we can improve
the future.

They...Back Then

During one of my workshops, I was caught off guard as I watched a participant's jaw drop to the floor in surprise. By the end of my Queer History lesson, she was crying tears of relief. This older woman with a military-style haircut, cropped with a tight fade, wearing an oversized plaid coat had clearly heard something she had never heard before—something that mattered deeply to her.

After I finished the workshop, I went over to chat with her. She told me that she had spent her whole life in a religious family. She had revealed to her family at a young age that she was a lesbian, and her loved ones had insisted her true self was an abomination, which only served to beat down her confidence and feed her self-doubt. She suppressed her true feelings for years while enduring an abusive, loveless straight marriage with a man her family had pressured her to marry. Recently, she had stopped denying her true self and come out as lesbian. But she was still finding it tough to find community and confidence.

She told me she was crying during my talk because it was the first time she had ever heard about anything in history that was Queer. Her family had persuaded her that being Queer was something *new*, so clearly it couldn't be valid. They used their lack of exposure to Queerness to justify holding her back from who she really is. Her family was convinced that being lesbian was a pathogen, an evil that had been "caught from rock 'n' roll" or something equally absurd. She told me she realized that if her parents had learned Queer history—that Queer people have always been here—then maybe they wouldn't have held her back so stubbornly.

The Untold Story of Queeroes

Even though we may not often hear their stories, there have been many Queer heroes, or, as I call them, queeroes, throughout time.

Nearly two thousand years ago, Roman emperor Hadrian's love for Antinous was not just personal—it was monumental. Homosexual relationships were not considered unusual in ancient Rome. After Antinous tragically drowned in the Nile, Emperor Hadrian mourned him publicly and lavishly. In his grief, Hadrian immortalized Antinous in a way no emperor had ever done before. He founded the city of Antinopolis in Egypt, a grand tribute to Antinous that became a center of art and culture. Across the Roman Empire, Hadrian commissioned countless statues and monuments bearing Antinous's likeness, ensuring his memory would live on for centuries. This wasn't just an expression of sorrow—it was a declaration of the profound bond between the two, one that carved their love story into history forever.

Other examples of queeroes include King Mwanga II of Buganda (Uganda), who held off European colonization longer than most African leaders, despite backlash for his relationships with male courtiers. Famed composer Pyotr Tchaikovsky, best known for *Swan Lake* and *The Nutcracker*, struggled with discrimination due to his sexuality in conservative Russia yet left behind love letters to men. And trailblazing entertainer Josephine Baker and iconic artist Frida Kahlo were also rumored to have been lovers. Both were known for their bisexuality, and reportedly met in Paris in the 1930s, but the details of their relationship remain speculative. And then there are literary legends like Gertrude Stein, Virginia Woolf, Walt Whitman, and Oscar Wilde, who each contributed to Queer culture in their own way.

In the early 1950s, Christine Jorgensen, an American actor and singer, was one of the first transgender individuals to capture the world's attention. After publicly undergoing gender-affirming surgery in Denmark—a bold and unprecedented step at the time—she returned to the United States to a media frenzy that both celebrated and scrutinized her transition. Jorgensen's public visibility challenged prevailing norms about gender and identity, opening up conversations that had long been taboo. Although she faced sensationalism and controversy, she paved the way for future generations of Queer people. Because of her fame she was one of the few Queer people who didn't go into hiding during the Lavender Scare (LGBTQ+ Life Lesson #4).

These are a few people for whom there is convincing evidence supporting their Queerness. But how many other queeroes have existed? We may never know, perhaps because they flew under the radar out of a desire for safety or perhaps because people never thought to look closely enough.

Invisible Queeroes

Human history seldom tells the stories of those who are marginalized and made invisible. This is why it's so difficult to trace the histories of feminism, Indigenous communities,

Queer people have always been here.

Black and other racialized groups, disabled people, and Queer communities. Many of those in power at the time didn't care to preserve these stories—or consider them worth saving. It's no coincidence we call it *his*tory rather than *her*story, *our*story, or *their*story.

In my public speaking and media work, I've had people challenge the Queer history I share, with comments such as, "But where's the exact proof?" And that's exactly the point—we'll *never* have complete Queer proof because so much of it has been erased, downplayed, or ignored. Instead, I'd like to make the bold claim that we need to be open to generously queering history, because if we don't, we might never see it at all.

That's why it's important to realize there were far more Queer people in history than is commonly recognized. The reason we don't know about many of them is that so many had to stay hidden—from a survival instinct or to protect their professional or social standing. This means the world around us, including all its achievements and gains, was shaped by Queer people far more than we'll ever fully realize.

There have also likely been Queer people whose great ideas never came to fruition because discrimination held them back. I imagine countless queeroes banging on doors, trying to show us how to save ourselves and make the world better, only to be ignored or silenced simply because they were Queer.

Where would we be now if society had listened to, accepted, and taken more seriously Queer ideas? What scientific innovations might have emerged, what lost species or natural places would remain, what art would move us, what teachings would have survived, and what truths would we already know if we had always listened to Queer people? We'll never know.

Here's the thing: When historians stumble across potential hints of Queerness, the mainstream narrative often bats them away, sticking to the comfort of a heterosexual or cisgender lens. Take Abraham Lincoln, for example. His life has been analyzed endlessly, but when C.A. Tripp's book suggested that Lincoln's relationships with men might have been something more, historians clutched their pearls and doubled down on the straight narrative. Tripp analyzed historical records, including Lincoln's reportedly loveless marriage to Mary Todd and his intimate, unusual relationships with men. For instance, Lincoln shared beds with male friends. Yes, that was more common in his era, but let's be real: This was Abraham Lincoln. He could have afforded his own bed. And yet mainstream historians wave it off.

Sure, there's no definitive proof Lincoln was Queer. What would that even look like? An X-rated daguerreotype? A diary entry saying, "Guess what, I'm gay"? Of course not. Any evidence would have been incriminating, career-destroying, or even life-threatening back then. So it's no surprise that it doesn't exist. The real kicker is that the scraps of evidence we do have—such as men sharing beds, letters brimming with infatuation, and unconventional relationships—are dismissed as "close friendships" or "different times." Meanwhile, a heterosexual marriage in an era when gay marriage wasn't even an option is somehow taken as conclusive proof of straightness.

So when people ask me for proof, I turn it around: Can you prove these historical figures were exclusively straight or cisgender? You can't. And yet the straight narrative marches on, unquestioned. Even if we're not prepared to definitively say someone was Queer, we should at least admit we can't definitively say they weren't. It's a double standard, plain and simple, and it erases the possibilities of Queer existence throughout history.

That's why, as allies and Queer people, we need to be willing to queer our own history when historians refuse to do it for us. If we don't, the stories that could have been ours will stay buried—and we've already lost far too many. We can't go back in time, but we can make things better by telling Queer stories now. To do that, we can frame Queer experiences and perspectives as a source of innovation and new ideas.

Queer Superpowers

There's something almost magical about being Queer that opens people's minds to innovation and problem-solving. Queer individuals are often forced to strengthen their solution-seeking muscles just by virtue of having to navigate a world built for straight and cis people. It's almost as if, in a world that tries to minimize them, Queer individuals turn around and magnify excellence just to fit in. Ironically, the very skills used to survive discrimination become the ones that help Queer people uplift and serve their communities.

Another reason Queer people are so adept at caring for and contributing to their communities is that, from a young age, they're forced to reflect on their place in the world. This self-awareness often develops into a fine-tuned empathy for those who are left out. Queer folks become highly sensitive to how the world affects people's feelings. The invisibility, suffering, and silencing that often come with being Queer foster an ability to recognize similar experiences in others.

That's why so many Queer people care about the world so deeply—because they know intimately what it's like to experience injustice. There's strong evidence that Queer people are more engaged in shaping the world around them than the average person. Studies show they are more likely to vote, volunteer, and get involved in community causes.

This is usually where I point out how lucky the rest of the world is that Queer people haven't decided to ditch all the discrimination and constant justification to form their own Queer nation. This hypothetical nation would be built on meaningful inclusiveness, dismantling inequities, and seeking innovation as a source of justice and well-being. Imagine those Queer foreparents (rather than forefathers) taking off to create a new homeland and leaving patriarchy, misogyny, unnecessary social constructs, and white supremacy behind. It sounds like a pretty fun place, doesn't it? Just think about the parties!

Queerness offers everyone—yes, including you—the permission to see history differently from how it's been told. Keep looking for and supporting "theirstory." When you do, you'll discover more about what it means to be diverse and beautifully human.

The Queer stories we tell don't always have to be history, either. Sure, it's important to honor the stories of the past, but there's also a huge gap when it comes to Queerness in the fantastical, fictional worlds of storytelling. Thankfully, that seems to be shifting, with more and more Queer representation popping up in media.

But have you noticed how that representation often comes with backlash? It's as if some people feel threatened if they're not the center of every story. And when something does include Queer or diverse characters, it's almost always talked about solely for that reason, then picked apart as though people are rooting for it to fail. Still, Queer creators and allies keep pushing forward, making space where there wasn't any before.

But here's the thing: We can't just sit back and hope media does all the work. Telling Queer stories in our everyday lives matters too. The next time you're telling a simple road trip tale to a kid, why not include a Queer character? You don't have to delve into identity crises or discrimination. Just make them an everyday person—maybe someone with a new name or different pronouns, or someone who loves a person of the same gender. That's it. No big speeches or lessons—just a casual part of the story.

And honestly, the kid listening might notice, or they might not. Either way, you're doing something beautiful. You're showing them a world where everyone gets to be included. You're helping them to grow up knowing that whoever they are and whoever they meet, it's all just part of the story. That's how we make Queerness not just something to fight for, but something that feels normal, everyday, and alive in the stories we share.

STORYTELLING IS an integral part of the human experience; it's how we pass on knowledge and understanding of the world. Many of us tell history and stories the same way they've always been told, but that leaves some people out—and reinforces the notion that they're less valid.

The Queer story is a beautiful one, and if we keep telling it that way, we might just save the world. That's next!

YOUR RAINBOW WISDOM TOOLKIT

When you tell your stories:

- remain open to the idea that historical figures may have been Queer—even if there's no "definitive proof";

- ask whether there's absolute proof someone wasn't Queer before dismissing the possibility;

- highlight Queer people's contributions and creativity instead of focusing solely on the discrimination they faced;

- include casual Queer characters or perspectives in your storytelling so diversity feels natural and expected; and

- keep telling Queer stories; by sharing these stories, you honor hidden heroes and inspire future generations to do the same.

SAVE THE QUEER COMMUNITY AND YOU SAVE EVERYBODY

Uplifting Queer voices
ignites the innovation,
compassion, and unity
the world needs.

Transitioning a Nation

Tamara Adrián was born in Caracas, Venezuela, in 1954, at a time when few could have imagined she'd become one of the country's most groundbreaking politicians. A lawyer by training, she earned her doctorate in France, where she not only honed her legal skills but also gained a fresh perspective on equality and human rights.

When she returned to Venezuela, Adrián built an impressive career as a lawyer and academic. But behind her professional success, she faced a deeply personal challenge: the struggle to legally change her gender. Venezuela's legal system made the process nearly impossible, forcing her to keep her birth name on official documents—a constant reminder of the systemic barriers she and so many others faced.

Adrián's transition in the early 2000s wasn't just personal; it became a political statement that highlighted the struggles of countless others without legal recognition. In 2015, she made history by becoming the first openly transgender person elected to office in Venezuela—and only the second openly transgender legislator in the Western Hemisphere. Yet, even when she registered her candidacy, she was forced to use her deadname, as Venezuelan law still prevents people assigned male at birth from legally adopting a female name. Her election to the National Assembly was a turning point for transgender representation and a source of hope for the LGBTQ+ community in Venezuela.

In 2023, Adrián broke even more barriers by becoming the world's first openly transgender candidate to run for the leadership of a country, putting her name forward in the presidential primaries. Despite the risks of opposing the Maduro regime, she campaigned on restoring democracy, addressing Venezuela's economic crisis, and fighting for equal rights for all marginalized groups. Her approachable personality and dedication to all Venezuelans have earned her widespread support, well beyond the LGBTQ+ community.

Adrián's advocacy doesn't stop with LGBTQ+ rights. She's been a powerful voice for gender equality, reproductive rights, and the well-being of Venezuela's most vulnerable citizens. She has also shone a spotlight on the country's political prisoners and crumbling health care system, which has a devastating impact on low-income families. Through the personal and professional challenges she's faced—including resistance to her push for gender identity laws—Adrián remains a symbol of courage and resilience. Her work continues to inspire and benefit not just LGBTQ+ individuals, but women, low-income families, and anyone fighting for equality and dignity in Venezuela's tenuous political climate.

Queer People Care (More)

Research by Eric Grollman shows that LGBTQ+ folks are more likely to recognize and empathize with other types of discrimination, such as racism or economic inequality. Why? Because we've been there—we know what it feels like to be left out. Queer people understand what it takes not only to imagine a better world but to step up and make it happen. There's this shared belief in the Queer Community that if we want things to change, we have to make it happen ourselves. No one's handing us progress on a silver platter.

Of course, social progress isn't unique to the Queer Community. Queer liberation has always worked alongside and benefited from other civil rights movements—like Indigenous resistance through Idle No More, Black civil rights, student activism, feminism, and anti-war protests. These movements influence and strengthen each other. Look at legends like Audre Lorde and James Baldwin—two giants in civil rights thinking. They were both Black and Queer, and they showed us how interconnected all our fights for justice are. As I said in LGBTQ+ Life Lesson #6, you can't isolate one part of a person's identity, because we are all multifaceted, intersectional beings. For example, the actions of a disabled, Black, trans woman—or her ally—help fight racism, ableism, and sexism while also supporting Queer liberation. That's how true liberation works—it uplifts everyone.

Queer liberation is full of examples of this interconnected fight for justice. Take the Black student sit-ins at "whites-only" lunch counters in Greensboro, North Carolina. Decades later, they inspired Queer couples in San Francisco to line up, year after year, to peacefully apply for marriage licenses they knew would be denied. And guess what? It worked. In 2004, Mayor Gavin Newsom stood with the Queer Community and started issuing same-sex marriage licenses, defying both the state's ban and Governor Schwarzenegger. That moment became a turning point, fueling the marriage equality movement worldwide. For many Queer people, me included, marriage equality was our "Stonewall," a milestone in Queer liberation that raised the bar for inclusion.

Queer people understand that progress takes action. The rights we enjoy today exist because someone before us stood up and fought for them. Social historian Nancy Unger points out that belonging to an oppressed minority teaches folks to see oppression more clearly and come up with solutions—not just for Queer issues but for everything from racism to environmental destruction. And studies back this up: Eric Swank's 2018 research shows LGBTQ+ folks are twice as likely as heterosexuals to join environmental movements and nearly three times as likely to support peace and anti-war efforts. Turns out, one of the gifts Queerness gives the world is more care—for each other and the planet.

The world has tried to box us in with outdated ideas of what we can be, but look how far we've come! We've already proven we can push past those limits. In the same way that we don't use floppy disks and rotary dial phones anymore, we can let go of the old "rules" about how we're supposed to live and think. To solve the big problems of our time—climate change, polarization, resource depletion—we need fresh ideas and bold, new ways of thinking. And who better to teach us that than Queer people? Queerness shows us how to break free from outdated norms and imagine what's possible.

Instead of getting our priorities straight, we are ready to get our priorities Queer. If we want humanity to thrive, we need to celebrate and nurture those who dare to be different, because that's where compassion and care live. Diversity isn't just nice to have—it's essential. Inclusion gives us the creativity and the imagination we need to tackle the hardest challenges and dream up a future we can be proud of.

We Need Diversity in Order to Survive

In this section, we're going to get a bit technical, dipping into some exciting ideas that scientists are exploring about the

Instead of getting
our priorities straight,
we are ready to get
our priorities Queer.

role that Queerness plays in the story of human evolution and biodiversity.

As any student of biology or ecology will tell you, the most vibrant ecosystems—where life flourishes, needs are met, and sustainability arises—require biodiversity. That's how nature worked before humans started drastically altering it; nature was in balance and abundance because of its diversity.

Biodiversity refers to the incredible variety of life on our planet, from the smallest bacteria to towering trees and majestic whales. This diversity is about not just the sheer number of species but also the genetic variety within those species and the myriad ecosystems they form. Each element of biodiversity plays a unique role in maintaining the balance and health of our environment. For example, bees pollinate crops, trees provide oxygen, mycelium mushroom networks spread nutrients and information across the forest floor, and wetlands filter water. Think of it as a giant, interconnected web where every strand strengthens the whole structure.

It becomes extremely difficult to live on Earth without biodiversity. When biodiversity disappears, it signals that the whole system is failing. Take, for example, An Gorta Mór, the Irish potato famine of the nineteenth century. An entire nation suffered when its main food crop was wiped out by blight. Starvation and disease spread rapidly, killing a million people and forcing another million to emigrate. Through overreliance on just one staple, nearly a quarter of the population disappeared. Just imagine what greater biodiversity might have contributed.

You may well be asking youself, what does any of this have to do with Queerness? Well, Queer people can be seen as contributing to human biodiversity. They offer humanity different categories, perspectives, and paths other than heterosexuality and the gender binary. This greater diversity in sexual and gender expression means that, as a species, we can more easily flourish. When the Queer Community thrives, all of humanity is healthier, because inclusion, safety, and openness are more available to everyone.

There's also some fascinating genetic research suggesting that Queerness may have played a role in how humanity evolved. Certain traits associated with same-sex behavior don't exist randomly—they appear to persist in human DNA because they indirectly boost the reproductive success of heterosexual relatives. In other words, Queer people might help humanity survive. Let me explain.

One well-studied phenomenon is the "fraternal birth order effect." Each older brother increases the likelihood that a younger male sibling will be gay. This is a scientific fact! But why would this be? Researchers think that hormonal shifts during pregnancy may influence the sexual orientation of later male children. But for what purpose? One theory suggests that while it is more likely that family DNA will be passed on through heterosexual siblings (because, generally, heterosexual folks are more likely to have children), a gay sibling—less likely to have their own children—is free to play a bigger role in supporting the upbringing of nieces, nephews, and niblings (a gender-neutral term) or taking care of aging parents. In this way, homosexuality might be nature's way of ensuring there are family members around who are not overwhelmed by the need to take care of their own children and can offer support to the family in other ways.

While this is just a theory, which is still being explored, it challenges the traditional view that Darwin's evolutionary theory of "survival of the fittest" is solely concerned with direct reproduction. Instead, this theory highlights the potential value of diversity within families, where each member can contribute to the group's survival and success in unique ways, and not necessarily solely through reproduction. It offers a fascinating glimpse into how the complex interplay of biology, Queer identities, and family dynamics might shape human development.

There's even more. There is a theory that some straight people carry the "gay gene," and it may help them be more successful. A study from the European Molecular Biology Organization found that genetic traits linked to same-sex behavior may express differently in heterosexual people who carry the gene, making them more socially skilled, more attractive, or even better parents. So even if Queer people don't pass on their genes directly, the "gay genes" remain in the human population because they offer advantages to the wider family. In other words, latent Queer genes, while not making every person Queer, can contribute to overall group success. So on behalf of the Queer Community, you're welcome!

And that's still not all. A study in *Nature Communications* suggests that same-sex behaviors benefit many mammal species, including primates, dolphins, and bison. The existence of same-sex behaviors within animal groupings has been linked to stronger social bonds, better cooperation, and increased survival. For instance, the presence of a gay member in a pod of dolphins or troop of primates lowers competition for mates, protects females and offspring from aggression, or helps the group stick together. The theory is that these same Queer contributions have served human evolution and progress as well. These dynamics benefit everyone, not just the individuals who engage in same-sex behaviors—another illustration of how diverse social interactions can help the entire community.

In short, Queerness isn't some genetic fluke. Instead, it may be one of nature's ways of keeping humanity adaptable and connected.

Despite all this evidence, some people still fall into the trap of thinking that Queerness is "unnatural" or that it is "taught." But every biologist will tell you: One rule of biology is that there are always exceptions. This is because life is unpredictable due to the complexity of living systems, evolution, and the influence of environmental factors.

I hope this research helps you understand that any effort to diminish Queerness in society attacks humanity's biodiversity as a whole. And when biodiversity suffers, we all suffer.

Diversity Is What We Need

When we put this all together—Queer people's ability to generate bold new ideas, their compassion for others, their heightened sense of environmental responsibility, and their genetic contributions that foster stronger, more cohesive communities—we see a promising picture of model citizenship, inspiring leadership, and even species survival.

Queer people expand human experience in new ways. By viewing Queerness as a source of fresh and daring ideas, we unlock humanity's potential to solve problems differently, and often better, than before. Add to that Queer folks' empathy and drive for social justice, and you basically have a dream résumé for the leaders our world needs.

And then there's the possibility that Queerness offers a biological advantage, helping us build healthier, more collaborative societies. The conclusion is clear: We need Queerness if we're going to thrive as a human species.

Collectively, the Queer Community is essential if we want a successful, united world of opportunity. If we truly desire a more just society, where everyone can reach their full potential, elevating Queer rights globally and supporting Queer

When humanity embraces the beauty of the Queer Community, it's ready to embrace its full potential.

leaders in positions of power will benefit us all. If we had more Queer representation in leadership, we'd have a planet more concerned with everyone's safety and well-being.

Right now, however, 29 percent of Queer people across the planet—that's 232 million people out of the estimated 800 million global total—are living in fear of imprisonment or being unfairly criminally targeted by their governments. A third of countries worldwide still criminalize Queerness. And this is not to mention all the places where legal protections exist but social acceptance still lags behind. Instead of just surviving, Queer people could be leading and contributing so much more, if only they were free and encouraged to do so.

United Through Queerness

There's Queer representation in every equity-deserving group: Indigenous, Black, people of color, disabled, unhoused, living in poverty, unsafe, hungry, or suffering. Queer folks bridge every aspect of humanity. If we save Queer people, we end up saving everyone. But why stop at saving? If we move beyond merely accepting and including Queer people, and instead elevate them to positions of power, leadership, and education, they could save the planet and all of us—if we let them.

As soon as humanity embraces the breadth and beauty of the Queer Community—along with its teachings, inspiration, and liberation—humanity will be ready to embrace its full potential. Until then, we will be missing out.

The biodiversity and compassion of Queerness are vital to humanity's greatness. When we're ready to include Queer communities wholeheartedly and unreservedly, humanity will attain the excellence it's destined for.

It will take work to repair the harm that excluding Queer people has caused the world. That exclusion drives many Queer people away from the spotlight or from community involvement, in self-defense. For everyone's benefit, we can begin nurturing Queer leaders among us, coaching and mentoring them as they find their own greatness. It's time to elevate Queer people and encourage them to guide us toward our highest potential. Support them, believe in them, elect them. The more we amplify inclusion in society, the better off we all are. Inclusion amplifies excellence.

If you want to save humanity, learn to love Queerness. If we want to be great, we have to let our Queerness shine. Our survival depends on it.

SOME POLITICIANS and leaders depict Queer people as a "deviation" or social weakness, but they're missing the bigger picture. Queer people bring advantages to our communities, including cohesion, innovation, and compassion, along with genetic and evolutionary benefits that strengthen our entire species.

The Queer experience offers valuable insights into achieving excellence—it's a road map available to everyone to help us realize our full potential. Throughout this book, we've explored how the Queer journey, guided by the 18 LGBTQ+ Life Lessons, serves as a powerful toolkit for recognizing and unlocking human strength. This strength comes from honoring who we truly are, rather than conforming to what the world tries to impose on us. When we embrace the Queer Community as a source of inspiration, we understand that we are all better off when we are true to ourselves. In this freedom, we shine brightly. And when each of us shines, humanity as a whole can reach its highest potential.

YOUR RAINBOW WISDOM TOOLKIT

When someone tries to convince you that Queerness "costs" society, look instead to Queer people for inspiration and leadership. Here are a few ways to do that:

- Support and elect Queer people who bring compassion, unity, and innovative solutions.

- Like nature, humanity thrives when diverse identities and perspectives are free to flourish, so let's celebrate diversity.

- Reject the "weakness" myth, because evidence shows that Queer communities strengthen society—socially, genetically, and ethically.

- Embrace our shared survival. Queerness crosses all demographics; by uplifting Queer rights, we uplift everyone.

- Foster widespread appreciation of Queerness. A world that fully includes Queer people unlocks its greatest potential for all.

SHINE BRIGHT WITH RAINBOW WISDOM

THANK YOU for joining me on this journey to foster Rainbow Wisdom. I hope learning these LGBTQ+ Life Lessons has helped you to better understand the Queer Community, your world, and yourself. As you reflect on what you've been reading and experiencing, remember that the Queer experience is simply a human experience—one that inspires every one of us, Queer or not, to be our best selves and seize the richness of life. Everyone is a gift. And though some might try to convince you otherwise, you deserve to value yourself for everything you bring. As I've said before, the best gift you can give the world is to be yourself and be inspired by diversity.

At its core, this journey is deeply personal. You have been invited to flex that muscle of intuition and authenticity to stand out, celebrating every strange, different, unusual, and unique part of you. When you amplify the uniqueness within, you amplify your gorgeousness, lighting up the world with a big, bold rainbow that inspires and transforms.

Self-affirmation and -celebration not only help you appreciate when you bust out of normal but also allow you to honor and cherish differences in everyone else. In a world that often pits us against one another, loving yourself is the most radical act of all. As our global drag mother and revolutionary icon RuPaul reminds us, "If you can't love yourself, how in the hell are you going to love somebody else?"

Confident self-acceptance spills outward, influencing our social circles and the wider community. You illuminate the shadows when you shine like a big, bold rainbow. It's no wonder that so many who aren't Queer seek refuge in Queer spaces and communities. Whether it's the lively energy of a Queer bar, the welcoming atmosphere of Queer beaches, or the inclusive spirit of Pride, people gravitate toward spaces where everyone is free to express themselves without the pressures of conforming to straight-cis norms. When you feel loved and safe, you radiate the kind of light that inspires others to embrace their own authenticity and live fully too.

Your journey of shining bright is not just about self-fulfillment, though. It's about breaking cycles and rewriting the rules passed down through generations. By showing up as your true self, you break free from fears of being too different and dare to create a better world for all of us. In living authentically, you contribute not only to your own growth but also to a vibrant and resilient community. A fulfilled person naturally enriches the lives of those around them, reinforcing the idea that the way to make the world a better place is simply by being your wonderfully unique self.

In exploring our sexuality or gender identity—or in witnessing others do so—we are reminded that there is no right or wrong way to be. Your identity is an internal reality, one that reflects what feels true and right to you. Instead of prescribing paths for others, we can all support each other's journeys, trusting that when a person embraces their truth, the world becomes a more authentic, radiant space. Shining bright like a big, bold rainbow not only brightens your own path; it also lights the way for others, fostering a collective glow of confidence and kindness, and an unyielding drive to be true to ourselves.

There will be moments when forging your own path feels daunting, especially when no one else has done it quite your way before. In these times, remember the strength of Rainbow Wisdom. When you commit to yourself rather than conforming to external expectations, you unleash the courage within you. If ever doubt or isolation creeps in, lean into your community. Those who recognize your brightness will reflect it back, amplifying it so that your whole world shines.

Queer people, LGBTQ+ people, Two-Spirit folks, and everyone else *on the rainbow* are a gift to humanity—a living testament to the beauty of living fully as oneself. And every single one of us, in our unique and authentic way, is also a gift to the world. By simply being you, you contribute to the diversity and richness of our planet, setting the stage for humanity to reach its full potential.

So, as you close *Rainbow Wisdom: 18 LGBTQ+ Life Lessons for Everyone*, remember that this life is your one chance to show up, to be authentic, and to shine as a big, bold rainbow. Shine bright. Live bright. Be you—this is what you were born to do.

Rainbow Wisdom:
18 LGBTQ+ Life Lessons for Everyone

These life lessons are a gift from the Queer Community to help the whole world reach its full potential. Take a picture of your favorite! Share them on social media, tag **@mischa.oak**, and help sprinkle Rainbow Wisdom around the world. And don't forget to visit **mischaoak.com** for free resources.

Raise the Bar: Skip the arguments. Elevate the conversation and stand by your values.

Congratulations! You're You! When someone shares good news, be a cheerleader and focus on the possibility.

Challenge Queer Fear: Fear doesn't make change wrong. Question the fear, not the change.

Save the Best, Leave the Rest: Curate the future of your dreams by carrying forward the best of the past.

Dive the Iceberg: When you face the unfamiliar, dive deeper to find the real story.

Why Fit in a Box When You Can Break It Down? Queer people show us that there is freedom in climbing out of those boxes.

Gender-Free Yourself: You are enough—no gender rules, no expectations, just you.

Joy Is Your Secret Weapon: Queer communities show us how celebration and joy fuel resilience and progress.

Stop the Surveillance: Respect means accepting that people should live freely, without policing.

Come Out as Yourself: Queer people show us the power of sharing our true self with the world.

You Don't Need to Be Fixed: Queer people aren't broken and don't need fixing—and neither does anyone else.

Lean Into Your Gateway Emotions: A gateway emotion is the spark of excitement that reveals the life you can have when you trust it.

Break Your Cornerstone Rules: Queer people inspire us to break cornerstone rules that no longer suit us.

Make the Future Nonbinary: The Queer experience reminds us that language is about embracing everyone's right to define who they are.

Stand Together: The Queer Community teaches everyone that solidarity in the face of confrontation is a profound act of love.

Inclusion Makes All Lives Better: When the world is designed with inclusion in mind, we make life better for everyone.

Tell More Queer Stories: Let's change the way we talk about humanity's past so we can improve the future.

Save the Queer Community and You Save Everybody: Uplifting Queer voices ignites the innovation, compassion, and unity the world needs.

ACKNOWLEDGMENTS

I AM GRATEFUL to all the Coast Salish Nations, whose lands have always been my home: the xʷməθkʷəy̓əm (Musqueam), Sḵwx̱wú7mesh (Squamish), səlilwətaɬ (Tsleil-Waututh), shíshálh (Sechelt), Snaw-naw-as (Nanoose), and Qualicum First Nations.

I stand on the shoulders of Queer heroes whose bravery, tenacity, and unapologetic joy cracked open the path we now walk. Their legacy fuels this work for justice and meaningful inclusion—and in their honor, we push forward, louder, bolder, and unstoppable. Many friends, teachers, students, and loved ones have inspired and encouraged me along the way. I wouldn't be who I am without you—thank you.

I will always carry gratitude for the Loran Scholars Foundation and Dr. Robert Cluett for believing in me and giving me wings.

A heartfelt thanks to the entire Page Two publishing team, including Carmen Ho, John Sweet, Viktoria Skaper, Rachel Seigel, Leslie Bootle, Taysia Louie, Adrineh Der-Boghossian, Trena White, and especially my gifted editor, Sarah Brohman, who believed in my ideas and supported me through the mammoth task of bringing my book to life.

I am forever inspired by those whose guidance makes my work possible: my writing doula, Lisa Thomas-Tench, who first noticed my story and helped me find my voice; my mentor, Bob Joseph, who showed me my path; my professors, Dr. Clar Doyle, who helped me realize I have something to say, and Dr. Sylvia Moore, who helped me see my place in the world.

I am endlessly grateful to my loved ones who make it all worthwhile: my husband, Sven Graaten, who has stood by my side every step of the way, even when I struggled to find my inner light; my mother, Dhyana Bartkow, who taught me how to be free and always trusted me to become who I am; my cheerleader and confidante, Shirra Wall; and my feline sidekicks, Oprah and Gayle, who kept me company as I wrote these words.

NOTES

LGBTQ+ Life Lesson #1: Raise the Bar

p. 20   *By early 2025, the Canadian province of Alberta:* Rob Drinkwater, "Groups Launch Legal Challenge Against Alberta's New Gender-Affirming Treatment Law," *Times Colonist* (Victoria), December 7, 2024, timescolonist.com/alberta-news/groups-launch-legal -challenge-against-albertas-new-gender-affirming-treatment -law-9923205.

p. 20   *the United Kingdom:* Brian Melley, "Britain Indefinitely Bans Puberty Blockers for Children with Gender Dysphoria," AP News, December 11, 2024, apnews.com/article/britain-puberty -blockers-banned-indefinitely-8993f4c3251aadd55521fa4ed9 87fc58.

p. 20   *twenty-six American states:* Summer Ballentine, "A Missouri Judge Says a Law Banning Surgery, Medications for Transgender Minors Is Constitutional," AP News, November 26, 2024, apnews.com/ article/transgender-law-missouri-courts-8a9cf71ac71853f16898c dd44bbe4704.

p. 20   *including Texas, Florida, and Georgia:* Associated Press, "Ohio Governor Signs Bill Limiting Bathroom Use by Transgender Students," *Politico,* November 27, 2024, politico.com/news/2024/ 11/27/ohio-governor-bathrooms-transgender-students-00192010.

p. 20   *every major medical organization, including the American Medical Association:* American Medical Association, "AMA Reinforces Opposition to Restrictions on Transgender Medical Care," press release, June 15, 2021, ama-assn.org/press-center/press-releases/ ama-reinforces-opposition-restrictions-transgender-medical-care.

p. 20   *and the American Academy of Pediatrics:* Alyson Sulaski Wyckoff, "AAP Reaffirms Gender-Affirming Care Policy, Authorizes

Systematic Review of Evidence to Guide Update," American
Academy of Pediatrics, August 4, 2023, publications.aap.org/
aapnews/news/25340/AAP-reaffirms-gender-affirming
-care-policy.

p. 20   *"life-saving health care for transgender people"*: HRC Foundation,
"Get the Facts on Gender-Affirming Care," Human Rights
Campaign, n.d., hrc.org/resources/get-the-facts-on-gender
-affirming-care.

p. 21   *transgender people make up less than 1 percent*: Jeffrey M. Jones,
"LGBT Identification Rises to 5.6% in Latest U.S. Estimate,"
Gallup, February 4, 2021, news.gallup.com/poll/329708/
transgender-identity.aspx.

p. 22   *transphobes continue to spread moral panic*: Adam Toy, "Puberty,
Gender Transitioning and Reversibility: Fact Checking Danielle
Smith's Claims," Global News, February 5, 2024, globalnews.ca/
news/10270448/puberty-gender-transitioning-reversibility
-fact-checking-danielle-smith.

p. 22   *a false narrative that these surgeries*: Daniel Dale, "Fact Check:
Trump Revives His Lie That Schools Are Secretly Sending
Children for Gender-Affirming Surgeries," WRAL News,
October 26, 2024, wral.com/story/fact-check-trump-revives
-his-lie-that-schools-are-secretly-sending-children-for-gender
-affirming-surgeries/21692064/.

p. 22   *not advised by global transgender gender-affirming care standards*:
E. Coleman et al., "Standards of Care for the Health of
Transgender and Gender Diverse People, Version 8," supple-
ment, *International Journal of Transgender Health* 23, no. 1
(September 2022), doi.org/10.1080/26895269.2022.2100644.

p. 22   *not happening to anyone under eighteen*: Kate Yandell, "Young
Children Do Not Receive Medical Gender Transition Treatment,"
FactCheck.org, May 22, 2023, factcheck.org/2023/05/scicheck
-young-children-do-not-receive-medical-gender-transition
-treatment/.

p. 22   *As of late 2024, nearly 40 percent*: HRC Foundation, "Map: Attacks
on Gender Affirming Care by State," Human Rights Campaign,
n.d., hrc.org/resources/attacks-on-gender-affirming-care-by
-state-map.

p. 22   *As of early 2025, fourteen American states*: Movement Advancement
Project, "Bans on Transgender People Using Public Bathrooms

and Facilities According to Their Gender Identity," MAP
website, updated April 15, 2025, lgbtmap.org/equality-maps/
nondiscrimination/bathroom_bans.

p. 22   *in many American states, including Kansas:* John Hanna, "Kansas
OKs Bill on Opting Kids Out of LGBTQ-Themed Lessons," AP
News, April 7, 2023, apnews.com/article/transgender-children
-kansas-schools-b249b1eb36409931a75eab1fbc80c15d.

p. 22   *Ohio:* Julie Carr Smyth and Samantha Henderson, "Ohio House
OKs Bill Making Schools Tell Parents of Transgender Children and
'Sexuality Content,'" AP News, June 21, 2023, apnews.com/article/
parents-rights-ohio-schools-education-gender-identity-b7fc1ba25
eb44c7808659231723aa3b7.

p. 22   *Florida's infamous "Don't Say Gay" legislation:* Florida Senate,
"CS/CS/HB 1557: Parental Rights in Education," State of Florida
website, March 29, 2022 (enacted July 1, 2022), flsenate.gov/
Session/Bill/2022/1557.

p. 22   *Even in the Canadian provinces of Saskatchewan and Alberta:* Kim
Clement, "Do No Harm: Concerns Raised over New Bill," Alberta
Teachers' Association, November 19, 2024, teachers.ab.ca/news/
do-no-harm; John Cairns, "Parents Bill of Rights Act passes in
Legislative Assembly," SaskToday.ca, October 20, 2023,
sasktoday.ca/highlights/parents-bill-of-rights-act-passes-in
-legislative-assembly-7715375.

p. 23   *in many states including Arizona:* Peyton Sorosinski, "New
Arizona Bill Would Require Schools to Notify Parents if Their
Child Changes Pronouns," *Washington Examiner*, February 6,
2024, washingtonexaminer.com/news/2840116/new-arizona
-bill-require-schools-notify-parents-their-child-changes-pronouns.

p. 23   *Indiana:* Geoff Mulvihill, "States Add Laws on Pronouns,
Sports for Transgender Students," AP News, May 5, 2023,
apnews.com/article/lgbtq-students-bathrooms-sports-pronouns
-e53a0e7ca87001f1b97139098ee0906f.

p. 23   *and North Carolina:* Emily Walkenhorst, "Wake School Board
Adopts New Parents' Law into Policy Books," WRAL News,
December 18, 2023, wral.com/story/wake-school-board-adopts
-new-parents-law-into-policy-books/21201510.

p. 23   *policies like these make kids more isolated:* Solcyré Burga,
"Anti-LGBTQ+ Policies Across American Schools Are Seriously
Impacting Queer Youth," *Time*, August 21, 2024, time.com/
7012940/anti-lgbtq-policies-impacting-queer-youth.

p. 23   *in 2024, of the 510,000 athletes:* Paul Steinbach, "Association President Tells Senate Panel There Are Fewer than 10 Trans Athletes Competing in NCAA," *Athletic Business*, December 19, 2024, athleticbusiness.com/operations/governing-bodies/article/15710780/association-president-tells-senate-panel-there-are-fewer-than-10-trans-athletes-competing-in-ncaa.

p. 23   *the* British Journal of Sports Medicine *found that transgender women:* Timothy A. Roberts, Joshua Smalley, and Dale Ahrendt, "Effect of Gender Affirming Hormones on Athletic Performance in Transwomen and Transmen: Implications for Sporting Organisations and Legislators," *British Journal of Sports Medicine* 55, no. 11 (2021): 577–83, doi.org/10.1136/bjsports-2020-102329.

p. 28   *according to the Canadian Pediatric Society:* Canadian Paediatric Society, "Gender Identity," *Caring for Kids*, last updated June 2023, caringforkids.cps.ca/handouts/behavior-and-development/gender-identity.

p. 29   *and the American Academy of Pediatrics:* Jason Rafferty, "Gender Identity Development in Children," HealthyChildren.org, last updated May 7, 2024, healthychildren.org/English/ages-stages/gradeschool/Pages/Gender-Identity-and-Gender-Confusion-In-Children.aspx.

LGBTQ+ Life Lesson #2: Congratulations! You're You!

p. 39   *Ellen D.B. Riggle's extensive research:* Ellen D.B. Riggle and Sharon S. Rostosky, *A Positive View of LGBTQ: Embracing Identity and Cultivating Well-Being* (Rowman & Littlefield Publishing Group, 2012).

LGBTQ+ Life Lesson #3: Challenge Queer Fear

p. 53   *The theory of falsification:* Karl Popper, *Logik der Forschung* (The logic of scientific discovery) (Springer-Verlag, 1935). Translated into English in 1959.

p. 55   *An Ipsos poll:* Chris Jackson, "Pride Month 2023: 9% of Adults Identify as LGBT+," Ipsos, June 1, 2023, ipsos.com/en/pride-month-2023-9-of-adults-identify-as-lgbt.

p. 57   *most permanent procedures such as gender-affirming genital transition:* E. Coleman et al., "Standards of Care."

LGBTQ+ Life Lesson #4: Save the Best, Leave the Rest

p. 65   *Alexander the Great was open about his romantic relationships:*
Athena Richardson, "Alexander the Great and Hephaestion:
Censorship and Bisexual Erasure in Post-Macedonian Society,"
George Washington University, August 27, 2018, scholarspace
.library.gwu.edu/concern/gw_works/w9505070k; Jeanne Reames,
"An Atypical Affair? Alexander the Great, Hephaistion Amyntoros
and the Nature of Their Relationship," *History Faculty Publications*
(1999), 17, digitalcommons.unomaha.edu/histfacpub/17.

p. 65   *some medieval Muslim societies and art forms:* Stephen O. Murray
and Will Roscoe, eds., *Islamic Homosexualities: Culture, History,
and Literature* (New York University Press, 1997); Khaled
El-Rouayheb, *Before Homosexuality in the Arab-Islamic World,
1500–1800* (University of Chicago Press, 2005).

p. 65   *Leonardo's potential Queerness:* James M. Saslow, *Ganymede in
the Renaissance: Homosexuality in Art and Society* (Yale University
Press, 1986).

p. 65   *the Christian church began heavily decrying:* John Boswell,
*Christianity, Social Tolerance, and Homosexuality: Gay People
in Western Europe from the Beginning of the Christian Era to the
Fourteenth Century* (University of Chicago Press, 1980).

p. 67   *The fear of being labeled a traitor/Communist:* Warren J. Blumenfeld,
review of *The Lavender Scare: The Cold War Persecution of Gays
and Lesbians in the Federal Government* by David K. Johnson,
Feminist Review 83 (2006): 159–61, jstor.org/stable/3874391.

p. 70   *Rabbi Elliot Kukla made history in 2006:* Elliot Kukla, "Ancient
Judaism Recognized a Range of Genders. It's Time We Did, Too,"
New York Times, March 18, 2023, nytimes.com/2023/03/18/
opinion/trans-teen-suicide-judaism.html; Rabbi Eli Kukla,
"A Blessing for Transitioning Genders," TransTorah, 2006,
transtorah.org/PDFs/Blessing_for_Transitioning_Genders.pdf.

LGBTQ+ Life Lesson #5: Dive the Iceberg

p. 78   *"Labels are not more than starting points":* Edward W. Said,
Orientalism (Pantheon Books, 1978).

p. 85   *"Before we can fight for each other":* Kalki Subramaniam, *We Are Not
the Others: Reflections of a Transgender Artivist* (Notion Press, 2021).

p. 85   *LGBTQ+ individuals make up about 9 percent:* Jackson, "Pride
Month 2023."

LGBTQ+ Life Lesson #6: Why Fit in a Box When You Can Break It Down?

p. 97   *In his memoir* Asylum, *Okporo details:* Edafe Okpop, *Asylum: A Memoir & Manifesto* (Simon & Schuster, 2022).

p. 97   *Kimberlé Crenshaw first introduced the concept:* Kimberlé Crenshaw, "Demarginalizing the Intersection of Race and Sex: A Black Feminist Critique of Antidiscrimination Doctrine, Feminist Theory and Antiracist Politics," *University of Chicago Legal Forum* 1989, no. 1 (1989): 139–67.

LGBTQ+ Life Lesson # 7: Gender-Free Yourself

p. 105 *Japan is experiencing a demographic crisis:* Associated Press, "Births in Japan Hit Record Low as Government Warns Crisis at 'Critical State,'" *Guardian*, February 28, 2024, theguardian.com/world/2024/feb/28/birth-rate-japan-record-low-2023-data-details.

p. 108 *Before the French Revolution, rich men and women:* Valerie Steele, ed., *Encyclopedia of Clothing and Fashion* (University of Toronto Press, 2013).

p. 109 *The eye-opening documentary* The Mask You Live In: *The Mask You Live In*, directed by Jennifer S. Newsom (The Representation Project, 2015).

p. 114 *In his illuminating TEDx Talk "Everyone Is Trans":* Ian Harvie, "Everyone Is Trans," TEDxDirigo, Portland, Maine, December 15, 2015, 11 min., 38 sec., youtu.be/0YeVt2kp_So.

p. 115 *the famous Milgram experiment:* Stanley Milgram, "Behavioral Study of Obedience," *Journal of Abnormal and Social Psychology* 67, no. 4 (1963): 371–78, doi.org/10.1037/h0040525.

p. 115 *A lesser-known follow-up experiment:* Jerry M. Burger, "Replicating Milgram: Would People Still Obey Today?" *American Psychologist* 64, no. 1 (January 2009): 1–11, doi.org/10.1037/a0010932.

p. 116 *Classic cartoons and old films frequently ridiculed or villainized characters:* Ashlee M. Woods, "Transgender People and the Cinema: A Tainted History of Color," *Nineteen Fifty-Six*, April 11, 2022, 1956magazine.ua.edu/transgender-people-and-the-cinema-a-tainted-history-of-color; *Disclosure: Trans Lives on Screen*, directed by Sam Feder (Disclosure Films, Field of Vision, and Bow and Arrow Entertainment, 2020).

p. 116 *a 14 percent dissatisfaction rate:* Valeria P. Bustos et al., "Regret After Gender-Affirmation Surgery: A Systematic Review and

Meta-Analysis of Prevalence," *Plastic and Reconstruction Surgery—Global Open* 9, no. 3 (March 19, 2021): e3477, doi.org/10.1097/GOX.00000000000003477.

p. 116   *a 20 percent dissatisfaction rate:* Michael J. DeFrance and Giles R. Scuderi, "Are 20% of Patients Actually Dissatisfied Following Total Knee Arthroplasty? A Systematic Review of the Literature," *Journal of Arthroplasty* 38, no. 3 (March 2023): 594–99, doi.org/10.1016/j.arth.2022.10.011.

p. 116   *a 21 percent dissatisfaction rate:* O. Adogwa et al., "Decisional Regret Among Older Adults Undergoing Corrective Surgery for Adult Spinal Deformity: A Single Institutional Study," *Spine (Phila Pa 1976)* 47, no. 8 (April 15, 2022): E337–E346, doi.org/10.1097/brs.00000000000004287.

p. 116   *having an extremely low regret rate:* Breanna Y. Jedrzejewski et al., "Regret After Gender-Affirming Surgery: A Multidisciplinary Approach to a Multifaceted Patient Experience," *Plastic and Reconstructive Surgery* 152, no. 1 (July 2023): 206–14, doi.org/10.1097/prs.00000000000010243.

p. 118   *According to the National Institutes of Health:* Jedrzejewski et al., "Regret After Gender-Affirming Surgery."

LGBTQ+ Life Lesson #8: Joy Is Your Secret Weapon

p. 123   *In the early hours of June 28, 1969:* Ed Pilkington, "The Riot That Changed America's Gay Rights Movement Forever," *Guardian*, June 19, 2019, theguardian.com/lifeandstyle/2019/jun/19/stonewall-50th-anniversary-night-that-unleashed-gay-liberation.

p. 123   *The exact identity of the woman who was the catalyst:* David Carter, *Stonewall: The Riots That Sparked the Gay Revolution* (St. Martin's Press, 2004).

p. 124   *Protesters sang "We Shall Overcome":* Garance Franke-Ruta, "An Amazing 1969 Account of the Stonewall Uprising," *Atlantic*, January 24, 2013, theatlantic.com/politics/archive/2013/01/an-amazing-1969-account-of-the-stonewall-uprising/272467/.

p. 124   *Marsha P. Johnson, a Black transgender woman:* The term "transgender" wasn't widely used in Marsha's time; Marsha described herself as a gay person, a transvestite, and a drag queen. She used she/her pronouns, though she is widely celebrated for contributing to the gender-nonconforming, genderfluid, and transgender movements. That work continues in her name with the influential

Marsha P. Johnson Institute. (New York Historical, "Life Story: Marsha P. Johnson (1945–1992)," NYHistory.org, n.d., wams .nyhistory.org/growth-and-turmoil/growing-tensions/marsha -p-johnson/.)

p. 124 *There are reports that she was among the first to fight back:* Carter, *Stonewall.*

p. 125 *she added the "P." to her name:* Carter, *Stonewall.*

p. 126 *By coming out publicly, Martin and Lyon:* GLBT Historical Society, "Primary Source Set: Phyllis Lyon and Del Martin," GLBTHistory .org, n.d., glbthistory.org/primary-source-set-lyon-and-martin.

p. 130 *"During the darkest days of the* AIDS *crisis":* Dan Savage, "Savage Love: Trump and Dump," *Portland Mercury,* January 21, 2025, portlandmercury.com/savage-love/2025/01/21/47609318/ savage-love-trump-and-dump.

LGBTQ+ Life Lesson #9: Stop the Surveillance

p. 136 *the panopticon, a type of institutional architecture:* Jeremy Bentham, *The Panopticon Writings,* ed. M. Božovič (Verso, 1995 [1787]).

p. 138 *According to The Trevor Project:* R. Nath et al., *2024 U.S. National Survey on the Mental Health of* LGBTQ+ *Young People* (The Trevor Project, 2024), thetrevorproject.org/survey-2024/.

p. 138 *According to the Centers for Disease Control and Prevention:* Nicolas A. Suarez et al., "Disparities in School Connectedness, Unstable Housing, Experiences of Violence, Mental Health, and Suicidal Thoughts and Behaviors Among Transgender and Cisgender High School Students: Youth Risk Behavior Survey, United States, 2023," *Mortality and Morbidity Weekly Report* (Centers for Disease Control and Prevention) 73, no. 4 (October 10, 2024): 50–58, cdc.gov/mmwr/volumes/73/su/su7304a6.htm.

p. 141 *Sociologist Eric Klinenberg emphasizes:* Eric Klinenberg, *Palaces for the People: How Social Infrastructure Can Help Fight Inequality, Polarization, and the Decline of Civic Life* (Crown Publishing Group, 2018).

p. 142 *Psychologist Carl Rogers found that practicing active listening:* Carl R. Rogers, *On Becoming a Person: A Therapist's View of Psychotherapy* (Houghton Mifflin, 1961).

p. 142 *trust builds stronger relationships:* Brené Brown, *Dare to Lead: Brave Work. Tough Conversations. Whole Hearts.* (Random House, 2018).

LGBTQ+ Life Lesson #10: Come Out as Yourself

p. 149 *up to 40 percent of Queer people stay closeted:* HRC Foundation, "Equality Rising: LGBTQ+ Workers and the Road Ahead," Human Rights Campaign, n.d., hrc.org/resources/equality-rising-lgbtq -workers-and-the-road-ahead.

p. 149 *Michael Bach calls this the* Curse of Constantly Coming Out: Michael Bach, *Alphabet Soup: The Essential Guide to* LGBTQ2+ *Inclusion at Work* (Page Two, 2022).

p. 149 *Google's Project Aristotle found that psychological safety:* Charles Duhigg, "What Google Learned from Its Quest to Build the Perfect Team," *New York Times Magazine*, February 25, 2016.

p. 149 *Rolls-Royce's "Being Like Me" initiative:* Sylvia Pfeifer, "Rolls-Royce Hardwires Inclusion into its Systems," *Financial Times*, November 19, 2024.

LGBTQ+ Life Lesson #11: You Don't Need to Be Fixed

p. 162 *sexual minority men put more energy into achievement*: John E. Pachankis and Mark L. Hatzenbuehler, "The Social Development of Contingent Self-Worth in Sexual Minority Young Men: An Empirical Investigation of the 'Best Little Boy in the World' Hypothesis," *Basic and Applied Social Psychology* 35, no. 2 (2013): 176–90, doi.org/10.1080/01973533.2013.764304.

LGBTQ+ Life Lesson #12: Lean Into Your Gateway Emotions

p. 178 *A study published in* Frontiers in Psychology: Geir Kirkebøen and Gro H.H. Nordbye, "Intuitive Choices Lead to Intensified Positive Emotions: An Overlooked Reason for 'Intuition Bias'?" *Frontiers in Psychology* 8, article no. 1942 (November 2017): doi.org/10.3389/ fpsyg.2017.01942.

p. 180 *following intuition can lead to success:* John M. Coates, *The Hour Between Dog and Wolf: Risk Taking, Gut Feelings, and the Biology of Boom and Bust* (Penguin Press, 2012).

LGBTQ+ Life Lesson #13: Break Your Cornerstone Rules

p. 189 *Indian transgender advocate Kalki Subramaniam:* Subramaniam, *We Are Not the Others.*

LGBTQ+ Life Lesson #14: Make the Future Nonbinary

p. 200 *In Alok's book* Beyond the Gender Binary: Alok Vaid-Menon, *Beyond the Gender Binary* (Penguin Workshop, 2020).

p. 200   *"The American ideal, then, of sexuality"*: James Baldwin, "Here Be Dragons," in *The Price of the Ticket: Collected Nonfiction, 1948-1985* (St. Martin's Press, 1985), 680-99.

p. 204   *In North America, many First Nations honored individuals:* Qwo-Li Driskill, "Stolen from Our Bodies: First Nations Two-Spirits/Queers and the Journey to a Sovereign Erotic," *Studies in American Indian Literatures* 16, no. 2 (Summer 2004): 50-64, doi.org/10.1353/ail.2004.0020.

p. 204   *In South Asia, the hijra community:* Religious Literacy Project, "The Third Gender and Hijras," Harvard Divinity School, 2018, rpl.hds.harvard.edu/religion-context/case-studies/gender/third-gender-and-hijras.

p. 204   *In precolonial Africa, the Igbo people:* Kenneth Nwoko, "Female Husbands in Igboland, Southeast Nigeria," *Pan-African Journal* 5 (2012): 69-82.

p. 204   *In Hawaii and Tahiti:* Libby Leonard, "Hawaii's Māhū—and Their Ancient History—Are Finally Re-Embraced," *National Geographic*, May 8, 2023, nationalgeographic.com/premium/article/hawaii-mahu-ancient-history-finally-re-embraced; Aleardo Zanghellini, "Sodomy Laws and Gender Variance in Tahiti and Hawai'i," *Laws* 2, no. 2 (2013): 51-68, doi.org/10.3390/laws2020051.

p. 204   *Meanwhile, in Samoa, fa'afafine:* Yoko Kanemasu and Asenati Liki, "'Let *Fa'afafine* Shine Like Diamonds': Balancing Accommodation, Negotiation and Resistance in Gender-Nonconforming Samoans' Counter-Hegemony," *Journal of Sociology* 57, no. 4 (2022): 806-24, toksavepacificgender.net/wp-content/uploads/2022/05/Kanemasu-Liki_2020_Let-fa-afafine-shine-like-daimonds.pdf.

p. 205   *In Chile, machis are Mapuche shamans:* Ana Mariella Bacigalupo, "The Struggle for Mapuche Shamans' Masculinity: Colonial Politics of Gender, Sexuality, and Power in Southern Chile," *Ethnohistory* 51, no. 3 (2004): 489-533, doi.org/10.1215/00141801-51-3-489.

p. 205   *In Southeast Asia, the Bugis people:* Sharyn Graham Davies, *Gender Diversity in Indonesia: Sexuality, Islam and Queer Selves* (Routledge, 2010), 30-47.

p. 205   *pre-Islamic Arabia acknowledged gender-nonconformity:* Everett K. Rowson, "The Effeminates of Early Medina," *Journal of the American Oriental Society* 111, no. 4 (1991): 671-93, doi.org/10.2307/603399.

LGBTQ+ Life Lesson #15: Stand Together

p. 211   *"When it comes to preventing AIDS"*: Ronald Reagan, "Remarks at the American Foundation for AIDS Research Awards Dinner," May 31, 1987, reaganlibrary.gov/archives/speech/remarks -american-foundation-aids-research-awards-dinner.

p. 212   *"The poor homosexuals"*: Igor Volsky, "Flashback—Buchanan: AIDS Is Nature's 'Awful Retribution' Against Homosexuality," ThinkProgress.org, May 24, 2011, archive.thinkprogress.org/ flashback-buchanan-aids-is-natures-awful-retribution-against -homosexuality-2049a2734cfb/.

p. 212   *There are accounts of nurses*: Maureen Hoch, "Essay: Treating the Earliest Cases of AIDS," PBS News, June 6, 2011, pbs.org/ newshour/health/health-jan-june11-volberding_06-06.

p. 217   *"If I didn't define myself"*: Audre Lorde, "Learning from the 60s," speech at Harvard University, February 1982, text available at BlackPast.org: blackpast.org/african-american-history/1982 -audre-lorde-learning-60s/.

p. 219   *"First they came for the socialists"*: United States Holocaust Memorial Museum, "Martin Niemöller: 'First They Came for…,'" Holocaust Encyclopedia, April 11, 2023, https://encyclopedia .ushmm.org/content/en/article/martin-niemoeller-first-they -came-for-the-socialists.

LGBTQ+ Life Lesson #16: Inclusion Makes All Lives Better

p. 235   *Research published by Cambridge University Press*: Luc Bovens and Alexandru Marcoci, "The Gender-Neutral Bathroom: A New Frame and Some Nudges," *Behavioural Public Policy* 7, no. 1 (2023): 1–24, doi:10.1017/bpp.2020.23.

p. 236   *The Williams Institute at UCLA School of Law*: Amira Hasenbush, Andrew R. Flores, and Jody L. Herman, "Gender Identity Non-discrimination Laws in Public Accommodations: A Review of Evidence Regarding Safety and Privacy in Public Restrooms, Locker Rooms, and Changing Rooms," *Sexuality Research and Social Policy* 16 (2019): 70–83, doi.org/10.1007/s13178-018-0335-z.

p. 236   *Research released by the University of British Columbia*: Elizabeth M. Saewyc et al., *"Students Feel Safer Here, and More Included": Evaluation of SOGI 123 in BC* (Stigma and Resilience Among Vulnerable Youth Centre, University of British Columbia, 2024), apsc-saravyc.sites.olt.ubc.ca/files/2024/10/SOGI-123-Evaluation -report-2024-10-08-FINAL.pdf.

LGBTQ+ Life Lesson #17: Tell More Queer Stories

p. 242 *Roman emperor Hadrian's love for Antinous:* National Museums Liverpool, "Antinous and Hadrian," LiverpoolMuseums.org, 2025, liverpoolmuseums.org.uk/antinous-and-hadrian; Caroline Vout, "Antinous, Archaeology and History," *Journal of Roman Studies* 95 (2005): 80–96, jstor.org/stable/20066818.

p. 242 *Famed composer Pyotr Tchaikovsky:* Rictor Norton, "Gay Love-Letters from Tchaikovsky to His Nephew Bob Davidov," Gay History and Literature, October 19, 2002, rictornorton.co.uk/ tchaikov.htm; Alexandra Orlova and David Brown, "Tchaikovsky: The Last Chapter," *Music & Letters* 62, no. 2 (1981): 125–45, jstor.org/stable/735028.

p. 243 *trailblazing entertainer Josephine Baker and iconic artist Frida Kahlo:* Emma Powys Maurice, "Celebrating the Life and Loves of Frida Kahlo, Mexico's Most Famous Bisexual and a Global Icon," *PinkNews*, July 6, 2023, thepinknews.com/2023/07/06/ frida-kahlo-birthday-bisexual-artist/.

p. 243 *Christine Jorgensen, an American actor and singer:* John T. McQuiston, "Christine Jorgensen, 62, Is Dead; Was First to Have a Sex Change," *New York Times*, May 4, 1989, nytimes .com/1989/05/04/obituaries/christine-jorgensen-62-is-dead -was-first-to-have-a-sex-change.html.

p. 246 *C.A. Tripp's book:* C.A. Tripp, *The Intimate World of Abraham Lincoln* (Free Press, 2005).

p. 247 *There's strong evidence that Queer people are more engaged:* Patrick J. Egan, Murray S. Edelman, and Kenneth Sherrill, *Findings from the Hunter College Poll of Lesbians, Gays and Bisexuals: New Discoveries about Identity, Political Attitudes, and Civic Engagement,* paper presented at the American Political Science Association, Hunter College CUNY, 2008.

LGBTQ+ Life Lesson #18: Save the Queer Community and You Save Everybody

p. 254 *Research by Eric Grollman:* Eric A. Grollman, "Sexual Orientation Differences in Whites' Racial Attitudes," *Sociological Forum* 33, no. 1 (2018): 186–210, jstor.org/stable/26625905.

p. 256 *Social historian Nancy Unger points out:* Nancy C. Unger, "Women, Sexuality, and Environmental Justice in American History," in Rachel Stein, ed., *New Perspectives on Environmental Justice: Gender,*

Sexuality, and Activism (Rutgers University Press, 2004), 46–60, doi.org/10.36019/9780813542539.

p. 256   *Eric Swank's 2018 research:* Eric Swank, "Sexual Identities and Participation in Liberal and Conservative Social Movements," *Social Science Research* 74 (August 2018): 176–86, doi.org/10.1016/j.ssresearch.2018.04.002.

p. 259   *"fraternal birth order effect":* Jacques Balthazart, "Sexual Partner Preference in Animals and Humans," *Neuroscience & Biobehavioral Reviews* 115 (2020): 34–47, doi.org/10.1016/j.neubiorev.2020.03.024.

p. 260   *A study from the European Molecular Biology Organization:* Andrea Rinaldi, "I Was Born This Way: New Research Confirms That a Mix of Prenatal Factors and Genetic Differences Could Explain Human Sexual Orientation," *EMBO Reports* 23, no. 6 (2022): e55290, doi.org/10.15252/embr.202255290.

p. 260   *A study in* Nature Communications: José M. Gómez, Adela Gónzalez-Megías, and Miguel Verdú, "The Evolution of Same-Sex Sexual Behaviour in Mammals," *Nature Communications* 14, article no. 5719 (October 2023): 1–12, doi.org/10.1038/s41467-023-41290-x.

p. 263   *29 percent of Queer people across the planet:* Saisuman Revankar, "LGBT Statistics by Country, Age, Sexuality and Facts," Electro IQ, January 6, 2025, electroiq.com/stats/lgbt-statistics.

LGBTQ+ GLOSSARY OF TERMS

2SLGBTQQIA+, 2SLGBTQ, 2SLGBTQI, 2SLGBTQ+, LGBTQ+, LGBTQ, LGBT, LGBTIQ, LGBTI, etc.: Inclusive umbrella initialisms and terms to encompass everything and anything that is NOT cisgender or heterosexual. The letters stand for 2S—Two-Spirit, L—Lesbian, G—Gay, B—Bisexual, T—Transgender, Q—Queer, Q—Questioning, I—Intersex, A—Asexual, and the "+" symbol includes other identities not specifically listed. These initialisms are often shortened in various ways, but they all aim to be as inclusive as possible.

AFAB: Assigned Female At Birth. This term is used to describe someone who was categorized as female at birth based on physical or biological characteristics. AFAB does not necessarily reflect a person's gender identity and should not be used to replace or stand in for "woman" or to describe cisgender women. It should be employed with care, as it can be misused to exclude or invalidate trans and nonbinary people. The term can be helpful when referring to specific biological or medical characteristics. *See also AMAB*.

Affirmed gender: One's true, self-recognized gender, which may differ from the sex assigned at birth. This term validates an individual's gender identity as real and legitimate, regardless of external perceptions.

Agender: A person who identifies as having either no gender or a neutral gender identity.

Ally: A person who actively supports LGBTQ+ rights and advocates for inclusivity, acceptance, and equality.

Alternative Gender-Neutral Pronouns: Used by individuals who do not identify strictly within the gender binary of he/she, him/her, and his/hers. These pronouns serve as alternatives to both traditional binary pronouns and the commonly used gender-neutral pronouns they/them/their. Common examples include, but are not limited to:

- **Xe/Xem/Xyr:** pronounced *zee, zem, zire*
- **Ey/Em/Eirs:** pronounced *ay, em, airs*
- **Per/Per/Per:** pronounced as in "person"
- **Ve/Ver/Vis:** pronounced *vee, vair, vees*
- **Ze/Zir/Zirs:** pronounced *zee, zeer, zeers*

Always use the pronouns someone requests to ensure inclusivity for nonbinary and gender-nonconforming individuals.

AMAB: Assigned Male At Birth. This terms refers to someone categorized as male at birth, though they may not identify as male. The term is not to be used to replace the concept of someone born as a cisgender man but rather is used sparingly to refer to specific biological or medical characteristics. *See also AFAB.*

Androgynous, androgynes: A gender expression that combines masculine and feminine qualities or appears gender-neutral.

Apogender: An identity for people who feel entirely removed from the concept of gender itself.

Aromantic: A person who experiences little or no romantic attraction and is often content with platonic relationships, though they may still be interested in physical intimacy.

Asexual, ace, ase: A person who does not experience sexual attraction or has little to no interest in sexual activity. Asexuality is distinct from celibacy, which is the deliberate abstention from sexual activity. Asexuality is one part of the broad spectrum of human attraction. It is also distinct from (a)romantic identity.

Bear: A term within gay culture to refer to a man who projects a rugged, masculine identity (often larger, hairy).

Bicurious, pancurious: A person exploring or curious about attraction to more than one gender.

Bigender: A gender identity involving two distinct genders, felt either simultaneously or alternating.

Bisexual, bi: A person who experiences attraction to both people of their own gender and people of a gender different from their own.

Butch: A gender expression or description characterized by traditionally masculine traits, often used by lesbians and other Queer individuals. Butch identity can encompass style, mannerisms, and self-perception, celebrating a broad and diverse expression of masculinity.

Ceterosexual: Attraction primarily to nonbinary or genderqueer people.

Cis-sexism: Acting with the assumption that everyone is cisgender. This behavior can be intended as discriminatory or it can be an unintentional act of ignorance/inconsideration.

Cisgender, cis: A person whose gender identity corresponds with their sex assigned at birth (e.g., a person who was assigned male at birth and identifies as a man).

Cisnormativity: The assumption that everyone is cisgender, marginalizing those who are not.

Coming out: Voluntarily making public one's sexual orientation and/or gender identity.

Cross-dresser, cross-dressing: A term for dressing in clothing or experimenting with gender expression not typically associated with one's gender; carries no implications of sexual orientation or gender identity.

Deadname: The birth name a transgender person no longer uses. Using their chosen name respects their affirmed gender and journey.

Deadnaming: The act of referring to a transgender or nonbinary person by a name they no longer use, often their birth or assigned name. Deadnaming can be harmful, as it disregards a person's identity, and can contribute to distress, invalidation, or discrimination.

Demisexual, demi: A person who experiences sexual attraction to someone only after having an emotional attraction to them.

Drag: A performance or act that challenges, impersonates, or entertains based on deconstructing or mocking gender norms. Drag has no implications regarding one's gender identity or sexual orientation.

Drag king: A person who impersonates masculinity or being a man; the performer can be any gender or sex. *See also Drag.*

Drag queen: A person who impersonates femininity or being a woman; the performer can be any gender or sex. *See also Drag.*

Dyadic: Refers to people whose physical and chromosomal traits align with commonly used categories of male or female, as opposed to intersex.

Feminine: A term describing qualities or expressions culturally associated with being female, though these vary across cultures and individuals.

Femme: A gender expression that emphasizes femininity, often used within LGBTQ+ communities to describe identity, style, and presence.

Furries: Members of a subculture centered around an interest in anthropomorphic animals—animals with human characteristics—often expressed through art, costumes, and role-play. Being a furry is not a Queer identity, though the community includes people of all sexual orientations and gender identities. For some, being a furry may involve a fetish or sexual element, but for many others it is primarily a creative, social, or artistic expression. The furry community reflects a wide range of motivations and experiences.

Gay, gae: A person who experiences attraction to people of the same gender as themselves. The term "gay" may be used by individuals of a diversity of genders but is often used to specifically refer to men who are attracted to other men. The term may also be used by nonbinary individuals attracted to men.

Gender: A person's identity and inner sense of being male, female, both, neither, or something unique. Gender is deeply personal and may not align with biological sex.

Gender-diverse: An umbrella term for a wide range of expressions, experiences, and identities for people whose affirmed gender does not align with the gender they were assigned at birth, including transgender, genderqueer, nonbinary, and other gender-based identities.

Gender dysphoria: The distress or discomfort that can arise when a person's affirmed gender does not align with the sex assigned at birth, or when they are perceived or represented in a way that contradicts their affirmed gender. This distress can manifest emotionally, socially, or physically and may vary in intensity from person to person.

Gender euphoria: The joy, comfort, or sense of rightness that arises when a person's affirmed gender is recognized, validated, or expressed in ways that align with their identity. This feeling can manifest emotionally, socially, or physically and may vary in intensity from person to person. Gender euphoria highlights the positive experiences of gender affirmation, such as being called by one's correct name or pronouns, wearing gender-affirming clothing, undergoing medical or surgical transitions, or being perceived in alignment with one's gender.

Gender expression: How someone expresses their gender outwardly, through clothing, style, behavior, or appearance. Gender expression can vary widely and is unique to each person.

Gender-free: A term used to describe the absence of gender or the rejection of gendered categories, labels, roles, or expectations. It can refer to individuals, spaces, or concepts that do not conform to or prioritize traditional gender categories, promoting inclusivity and neutrality.

Gender identity: An individual's deeply held sense of their own gender, which can be male, female, both, neither, or somewhere on the gender spectrum, distinct from biological sex.

Gender-neutral: A term for language or structures that do not assume or prescribe gender.

Gender-nonconforming: A term referring to people who do not conform to society's expectations for their gender roles or gender expression.

Genderfluid: A gender identity that can change over time, moving between different expressions or identities.

Genderqueer: A term for people whose gender identity is beyond the binary, often embracing fluid, nontraditional gender expressions.

Greysexual: A term for people who experience romantic or sexual attraction infrequently or in limited circumstances.

Heterocisnormativity: The assumption that being heterosexual and cisgender is the default or "normal" state, which marginalizes LGBTQ+ identities by reinforcing narrow expectations around gender and sexuality.

Heteronormativity: The assumption that heterosexuality is the default or "normal" sexual orientation, often leading to societal expectations and structures that marginalize LGBTQ+ identities and relationships.

Heterosexism: A system of attitudes, bias, and discrimination in favor of female-male sexuality and relationships; the assumption that everyone is, or should be, heterosexual; or the belief that heterosexuality is inherently superior to Queerness.

Heterosexual, hetero: A man who experiences attraction to a woman or vice versa. Also referred to as "straight."

Homophobia: Negative bias, fear, or aversion toward gay or lesbian individuals, which can lead to harm, discrimination, or exclusion.

Homosexual: A person who experiences attraction to people of the same gender as themselves.

Indigiqueer: A term used to refer to the Indigenous Queer community and as a specific individual identity. This term was coined by filmmaker TJ Cuthand and popularized by writer Joshua Whitehead to create specific language for those within the Indigenous Queer community who may wish to distinguish themselves from the spiritual and traditional aspects of Two-Spirit identities.

Intersex: A person with natural variations in sex characteristics such as anatomy, chromosomes, or hormone function that don't fit widely used binary definitions of male or female.

Latinx: A gender-neutral term for people of Latin American descent, embracing all gender identities.

Lesbian: A person who identifies as a woman and experiences attraction to people of the same gender. This term may also be used by non-binary people attracted to women.

LGBTQ, LGBTQ+, LGBT: *See 2SLGBTQQIA+.*

Masc: A gender expression that emphasizes masculinity, often used within LGBTQ+ communities to describe identity, style, and presence. *See also Butch.*

Masculine: A term describing qualities or expressions culturally associated with being male, though these vary across cultures and individuals.

Misgendering, misgender: The act of referring to or addressing someone in a way that does not align with their affirmed gender, such as using incorrect pronouns, names, or gendered terms. Misgendering disregards a person's identity and can cause emotional, social, or psychological harm.

MSM, Men who have sex with men: Not every man who engages in sexual intimacy with other men will identify as gay or bi. MSM is a term that originated in health care settings to ensure the same considerations used for gay and bi men (e.g., barrier-free services) are available to these men as well. There is a higher prevalence of MSM in rural communities and congregate living settings, such as prisons or work camps.

Neuroqueer: A term at the intersection of Queerness and neurodivergence, often challenging traditional gender norms.

Nonbinary, enby, NB: An umbrella term to reflect a variety of gender identities that are not exclusively male or female. Identity terms that may fall within this category include genderqueer, agender, genderfluid, or pangender.

Omnisexual: A sexual orientation involving attraction to all genders.

On the rainbow, rainbow family, in the rainbow: Casual phrases representing the diverse identities within the LGBTQ+ community.

Outing someone: Accidentally or intentionally publicly revealing another person's sexual orientation or gender identity, the fact that they are transgender, and/or their relationship status without their permission. This can cause social, physical, emotional, or economic danger for the person being "outed." Outing someone can sometimes be done as an act of hate.

Pancurious: *See Bicurious.*

Pangender: A gender identity encompassing many or all genders, reflecting a broad, inclusive view of gender.

Pansexual, pan: Describes attraction to people regardless of gender. For pansexual people, gender does not factor into their attraction. This is distinct from bisexual, which refers to a person who experiences attraction to both people of their own gender and people of a gender different from their own.

Passing: The experience of being perceived by others as a particular gender, often aligning with one's affirmed gender. While passing can bring feelings of safety or validation, it is not a requirement for fulfillment, success, or self-worth as a Queer person. The pressure to "pass" can reinforce harmful societal expectations rooted in cisnormativity, forcing individuals to conform to traditional gender norms.

Polyamorous, polyamory, poly: A form of ethical non-monogamy. Polyamory is the practice or ability to maintain more than one romantic and/or sexual relationship simultaneously. Consent and open communication are key aspects of polyamory. Not all polyamorous individuals will be in multiple relationships at all times, and this identity often includes other orientations, such as bi, pan, hetero, etc.

Pronouns: Terms used to refer to someone in place of their name, like he (him/his), she (her/hers), or they (them/their), corresponding to their gender identity. People may use various combinations of pronouns that most suit their identity, e.g., she and they. They/them/their are commonly used as gender-neutral singular pronouns to reflect experiences outside the gender binary of male or female. Some communities have also introduced new pronouns to reflect gender diversity, such as xe. *See also Alternative Gender-Neutral Pronouns.*

QTIBPOC, QTBIPOC, QTIIBPOC, QTIBIPOC: An acronym for Queer, trans, and intersex people of color, specifically highlighting racialized members of the Queer Community. The letters represent: Q—Queer, T—Transgender, I—Intersex, I—Indigenous, B—Black, POC—People of Color. QTIBPOC individuals often face intersecting forms of oppression related to race, gender, sexual orientation, and more, within both Queer and non-Queer communities.

Queer: A reclaimed umbrella term for sexual orientations and gender identities outside cisgender and heterosexual identities. It's a positive, inclusive identity for many in the LGBTQ+ community. Queer theory emerged from 1990s lesbian, gay, and gender studies. The term "Queer" was historically used as a pejorative term but was then reclaimed. Queer theory is a field of study that examines and critiques society's definitions of gender and sexuality; it aims to challenge traditional assumptions and social inequality and deconstruct what is considered "normal" culture. The term "Queer" can be applied to other fields to infer a similar deconstruction of widely held assumptions, i.e., Queer ecology, Queer urban planning, etc.

Queerphobia: Negative bias, fear, or aversion toward Queer, homosexual, or gender-diverse individuals, which can lead to harm, discrimination, or exclusion.

Questioning: An umbrella term for the process of discovering, feeling uncertainty about, or reconciling one's sexuality or gender identity.

Sapphic: Describes attraction between women or those of feminine identities, rooted in Queer women's culture and history.

Sex, anatomical sex, biological sex: A classification, usually assigned at birth, based on anatomy, hormones, and chromosomes, typically male, female, or intersex.

Sexual orientation, sexuality: Describes whom someone is attracted to romantically or sexually, covering identities like gay, lesbian, bisexual, pansexual, asexual, and heterosexual.

SOGI, SOGIE, Sexual Orientation and Gender Identity (Expression): Unlike the initialism 2SLGBTQ+, SOGI is a subject or topic, not a list of specific identities. It is an inclusive term relevant to all individuals, and includes all gender identities and sexualities, including lesbian, gay, bisexual, transgender, Queer, Two-Spirit, heterosexual, cisgender, and more.

Straight: *See Heterosexual.*

Therian, Therianthrope: Someone who identifies, in a non-physical way, as having an intrinsic connection to a specific non-human animal. This connection can be spiritual, psychological, or philosophical, and Therians may experience shifts in mindset, behavior, or instincts that align with their identified animal. Therianthropy differs from furries, as it is based on personal identity rather than role-playing or artistic expression. Common types of Therians include wolves, big cats, and other natural animals, though any real-world animal can be a theriotype. Unfortunately, some bad-faith actors online have tried to conflate Therians with trans people in order to discredit both groups, often as part of broader anti-LGBTQ+ rhetoric. However, Therians themselves do not claim to be transgender solely by virtue of their Therian identity, and many Therians are also cisgender.

Third gender: A gender identity that is neither male nor female, existing outside the binary.

Trans man: A gender identity describing someone assigned female at birth who aligns most closely with the cisnormative binary label of man.

Trans woman: A gender identity describing someone assigned male at birth who aligns most closely with the cisnormative binary label of woman.

Transfeminine: A gender identity describing someone assigned male at birth who aligns more closely with femininity. They may or may not describe themselves as a trans woman or as nonbinary.

Transgender, trans: An umbrella term for a wide range of experiences and identities for people whose affirmed gender does not align with the gender they were assigned at birth. *See also Trans man, Trans woman, Transfeminine, Transmasculine, and Transsexual.*

Transition: The personal process through which transgender individuals may change their gender expression, appearance, or physical traits. Transitioning can include social aspects (like name, appearance, and pronouns), medical steps (such as hormone therapy), and surgical options. Each journey is unique, and there is no single "correct" way to transition.

Transmasculine: A gender identity describing someone assigned female at birth who aligns more closely with masculinity. They may or may not describe themselves as a trans man or as nonbinary.

Transphobia: Negative bias, fear, or aversion toward transgender or gender-diverse individuals, which can lead to harm, discrimination, or exclusion.

Transsexual: An individual who transitions from their sex assigned at birth to align with their affirmed gender identity, in a process that may include medical or surgical changes. Transsexual people are part of the broader transgender community.

Two-Spirit, two-spirited, 2S: A pan-Indigenous term used by some Indigenous people to honor diverse or fluid gender identities and sexual orientations rooted in personal Indigenous traditions such as spirituality, connection to traditional teachings, or the land. Coined by Cree Elder Myra Laramee, the term often reflects precolonial understandings of gender fluidity, sexuality, and spirituality that vary across Indigenous nations. It is reserved for Indigenous people and reflects cultural roles and identities that colonial systems tried to erase.

ABOUT THE AUTHOR

MISCHA OAK (he/him) founded *LGBTQ Inclusion Training* to improve the lives of 2SLGBTQ+ people and support meaningful diversity and inclusion within organizations.

Mischa delivers transformative talks worldwide, guiding leaders, teams, and communities toward reaching their full potential through meaningful 2SLGBTQ+ inclusion. His celebrated TEDx Talk and keynotes are known for empowering people to bust out of normal to think and act in new ways.

He is a leader in SOGI Education, providing school boards, educators, governments, care providers, service providers, and communities with training and guidance on professional allyship and empowering inclusion—to foster life-changing progress.

Mischa believes inclusion amplifies excellence for everyone and that the Queer Community offers invaluable lessons that enrich humanity.

With over twenty years of experience as an educator and 2SLGBTQ+ advocate, Mischa holds a Master of Education in Social Justice Curriculum, Teaching, and Learning. He gained international recognition as part of the first wave of legal same-sex marriages in the world, featured on the reality TV series *My Fabulous Gay Wedding*. His involvement in the Queer Liberation movement propelled his lifelong advocacy, including expanding transgender and Queer inclusion in Canadian schools during his seventeen-year teaching career.

Mischa Oak is a Loran Scholar and an alumnus of Queen's University, the University of Toronto, and Memorial University.

HELP SHARE RAINBOW WISDOM BY MISCHA OAK

LGBTQ+ Life Lessons benefit everyone. Thank you for reading and joining the Rainbow Wisdom movement! As a thank you, please visit **mischaoak.com** for some free gifts and resources.

Please Share the Book

- Gift this book to a friend, a colleague, or anyone who wants to be a more confident ally.

- Share it with someone who has recently come out or has a loved one who has.

- Give it to those who may have questions or misconceptions about the LGBTQ+ community.

- Purchase copies for your team to foster inclusion and understanding. Bulk discounts and special offers available—contact us at **info@mischaoak.com**.

- Post pictures of the book on your favorite socials and tag **@mischa.oak**.

Stay Connected with Mischa Oak at mischaoak.com

- Subscribe to *LGBTQ+ Life Lessons for Everyone*.

- Watch Mischa's TEDx Talk.

- Book Mischa for your event. Bring a transformative keynote or fireside chat to your conference.

- Offer Mischa's LGBTQ Inclusion Training. Empower your team with confidence, strategies, and understanding.

- Shop the LGBTQ+ & Ally Merch Store. Get your ally sticker and merchandise now to shine bright and show you care.

@mischa.oak · @mischa-oak · @mischa.oak

Leave a Review

If you enjoyed *Rainbow Wisdom: 18 LGBTQ+ Life Lessons for Everyone*, please take a moment to leave a review on your favorite book retailer's site. Your words help amplify the message and move humanity forward. **Thank you for your support!**